ROY SHAW
UNLEASHED

ROY SHAW
UNLEASHED

KATE KRAY

JOHN BLAKE

Published by John Blake Publishing Ltd,
3, Bramber Court, 2 Bramber Road,
London W14 9PB, England

First published in paperback in 2004

ISBN 1 84454 088 X

British Library Cataloguing-in-Publication Data:

A catalogue record for this book is available from the British Library.

Design by ENVY

Printed in Great Britain by Bookmarque

1 3 5 7 9 10 8 6 4 2

Papers used by John Blake Publishing are natural, recyclable products made
from wood grown in sustainable forests. The manufacturing processes conform
to the environmental regulations of the country of origin.

Picture reproduced by kind permission of Chris Wood.

Every attempt has been made to contact the relevant copyright-holders,
but some were unobtainable. We would be grateful if the appropriate
people could contact us.

CONTENTS

AUTHOR'S NOTE

Roy Shaw has always been a private man –
he holds his cards close to his chest and has never
bared his soul to anyone. Until now. I would like
to thank him for putting his trust in me and being
so open and honest.

Kate Kray, 2004

DEDICATION

I would like to dedicate this book to Mandy Bruce,
who taught me everything I know about writing.
Mandy passed away in April 2003. She was a dear
friend and will be sorely missed.

ACKNOWLEDGEMENTS

Thank you to all Roy's friends for taking part.
Also, Steve 'Nostrils' Rolls, Al and Elaine Irvine,
St Bernard's Animal Sanctuary, the many researchers
who helped me look for Dorothy. A big thank you to
Joan Bentley and, of course, Leo.

INTRODUCTION

ROY SHAW. Harder than life, meaner than death. A vicious fighter with a vicious temper.

Watch out when he gets riled, his eyes narrow, his fists clench and he tears in. You'll hear bones crack, smell blood and see guts gush out and spill across the floor. Roy has been described as Britain's most violent man. It's an understatement. But there's a man behind the legend, the gangster who has lived an incredible life from bare-knuckle fighting to major crime, extreme violence and championship title fights. I wanted to find out more about him, about the aggression – how did Roy Shaw come about? Was he a kid from the back streets who was dealt a rough hand? Or did Roy discover something about himself and learn how to use it?

Did his natural talent for fighting become an addiction worse than any drug, a crazy fix of pain, power and aggression.

INTRODUCTION

They say that talk is cheap, but the stories I'd heard about Roy Shaw were unlike anything I'd come across before – they ranged from the truly horrific to the grisly, the gruesome and the bizarre. But, although Roy doesn't let on, I thought there had to be a gentler side to him and I was determined to find it. I meant to peel off the layers of savagery and violence and see what was underneath!

I met Roy's friends and realised that they all have a different tale to tell. I talked to the boxing fraternity first. More than anyone, they should know if he'd got what it takes. What sort of a fighter was he? Did he have what it takes? Very few boxers make champion – could Roy Shaw have made it to the top? Maybe ... if a little bit of armed robbery, murder and gratuitous violence beyond your most hellish nightmares hadn't got in the way!

London is his territory and Roy became one of the coolest, quietest and most dangerous of the East End villains. Physically powerful and with biceps like marble pillars, when anyone crossed him the rage built up, exploded and then ... whack!

Roy was unable to control his murderous rage, bouncing around the mean streets and rubbing shoulders with the bad guys like a powder keg waiting to go off. Everybody knew Roy Shaw and feared him – but with the fear came absolute respect.

Roy grew up fast; he wanted money and nothing was going to stop him getting it. He was strong, super fit, fearless and impervious to pain. A diabolical mix of ruthlessness and terror. In his world, the rules didn't apply – to him, anyway.

He wanted money – he took it. He wanted women – he had them. Everything was within reach of those steely nerves and iron fists.

Until ... a raid on a bank van went wrong, his luck ran out and his life went into free fall. Within a few short weeks, he was swapping the soft leather seats in his new Mercedes for the bare walls of a prison cell.

His life was tumbling into free fall, one bad luck domino knocking another down in a chain to hell. Nothing could stop it.

When he was sentenced to be imprisoned for 18 years, he had nothing to lose and punched and kicked and fought his way through his sentence. Something inside him wouldn't give up or give in.

I don't know whether it's good or bad but I don't think we'll ever see men like Roy Shaw again. Men who are forged in a cold steel mould, tempered with determination and polished with fury. But now the gladiators are gone and we live in more civilised times.

Roy is still a legend, our last 'out-of-time' fighter – a hero or a villain? Who knows. He is a man who doesn't know how to give in or give up – he settles his scores the only way he knows – with his fists.

As I talked to him and listened to what other people had to say, I realised that he is still the same today. If you need someone on your side, he is the best. But have it the other way and you will encounter an adversary from hell. ' "Vengeance is mine," sayeth the Lord' – and Roy Shaw. He never forgives, he never forgets. Roy lives without rules and he will tell you, without holding anything back, that there is blood on his hands.

He acts first and doesn't think about it later. Even in his no-holds-barred world, he's a ruthless bastard who doesn't hesitate to wade in and who can fight his way out of anything.

It's been a raging roller-coaster life, high living then off the rails into black tunnels of despair – from maximum-security lock-ups, torture and insanity, this has been a career like no other, a life steam-rollering without regret through paths of pain and retribution. If Roy looks your way, cross yourself and step back into the shadows. Make no mistake, he is a bringer of fear and death. Consequence and regret are words that mean nothing to him.

But let's take another look at Roy Shaw now. There's a mansion in millionaire's row, a shiny red Bentley parked up in the drive and enough money in the bank to enable him to buy anything he wants.

Has he left his past behind? How come he's made it – swapped clanging cell doors and cold bare walls for winters in the sun, top-marque motors, expensive real estate, fine wines and beautiful women.

He's a wealthy businessman, a connoisseur, a property entrepreneur.

After ten years inside the toughest prisons in the country, Roy has reinvented himself, changed from hardened con into the man with the Midas touch. A change of life so dramatic that it brings more questions than answers.

How could a man so violent, so ingrained in crime

become this geezer parking his Bentley outside a posh restaurant and dining out with Miss Supermodel draped all over his arm like a cashmere overcoat?

Rich, civilised, successful? How come?

Roy started out as one of the most promising professional boxers of his day, an iron-fisted opponent who slugged it out to win fight after fight. They couldn't put him down. The glittering prizes of a fabulous boxing career were on the horizon – he was set for the big time ... except for one or two little problems. Roy can sort out most things but he couldn't change his past. Roy had been living in a hard knocks world where crime was the name of the game and villainy was a way of life. Boxing was the escape ticket, and Roy was becoming well known, well paid and seriously ambitious ... until his little bouts of naughtiness caught up with him, and his periods of board and lodging in Wormwood Scrubs and a few others of Her Majesty's prisons came to the knowledge of the British Boxing Board of Control.

Fate can be a ruthless bastard, too, and suddenly intervened and kicked him back to where he'd come from – Roy was devastated when he was refused a licence to box, when his brilliant career bounced off the ropes – eight, nine, ten ... you can't box again ... you're out ... it was a knockout blow even he couldn't get up from.

It took a long time to get over this devastating decision. A tiny kernel of pain is still there. What if ...?

Roy might have been down but he wasn't out and if he couldn't fight within the rules, he'd fight outside them –

like a volcano about to spew molten lava – all the pent-up aggression had to go somewhere and the brutal unlicensed fight game became his new explosive territory. Roy became one of the most feared fist-fighters ever. His raw punch-ups culminated in the famous match between him and Lenny McLean – a fight that is still talked about today as one of the bloodiest ever. No one could go the distance with Lenny, who was a giant of a man and as tough as they come. Roy did. No one could put Lenny down. Roy did. Lenny couldn't be beaten. But Roy beat him and smashed him to a pulp until the ring was slippery with blood – and Roy was the undisputed British Unlicensed Boxing Champion. No matter what their reputation – the reality is that he chews them up and spits them out.

How does he do it? Is it the look – the way he stares you down? Those piercing and unblinking shark-blue eyes never flinch. Is it an attitude of mind? Does anyone know what Roy Shaw is really about? Does anyone understand him? How can you tell what he's thinking?

The simple answer is – you can't. The mask never slips, he's weighing you up and counting the odds – it's not until his face cracks into a smile that you can relax with a sigh of relief.

Almost everyone I spoke to about Roy said the same – if you get on the wrong side of him you can expect trouble. Watch you don't ever cross him. Why?
Because everyone who has done ...

I knew that, all through his life of crime, Roy has been respected by every top gangster in the country – the twins

Ronnie and Reggie Kray, Jack 'The Hat' McVitie, Frank 'Mad Axe' Mitchell and Harry Roberts, the cop killer. The list is endless. Roy is completely without fear and, in the dark, shadowy underworld, Roy is a legend. His ability to take punishment and come back is without equal. His whole life has been based on fight, fight, fight – this man doesn't know what it means to back off or step aside. Roy became so aggressive and dangerous that no prison in the country could handle him, not even Broadmoor Hospital for the Criminally Insane.

* * *

I was on my way to see him and wondering if he'd changed since we last met when I interviewed him for his bestselling autobiography *Pretty Boy*. Roy was one of the toughest guys I'd ever come across. Although he'd always behaved like a perfect gentleman towards me, I could always sense the anger and hostility bubbling away beneath the surface. I was curious to know what Roy had been up to since he was released from prison. Had 'Pretty Boy' learned his lesson? Was he still dabbling in lots of naughty things that he didn't really want to talk about?

I knew he was as vengeful as ever. One of the first things he did when he came out was to sort out his ex-wife's boyfriend. A quiet chat over a pint? I don't think so. He chucked the bloke over the balcony. Three floors up. After the life he's lived, the villainy, the prison, the years in Broadmoor, how could anything change?

Or could it? When he was finally released after a lifetime of crime, Roy set about becoming a successful businessman. Against all the odds, he succeeded.

You can take the man out of the fight but you can't take the fight out of the man and his reputation as a hardened enforcer and man to respect was well established.

Nearly every gangster or villain I've met when I've been writing my books would, at some stage, mention him. They all had a different story to tell. Mention the name Roy Shaw and geezers who'd eat their granny for breakfast would go pale, their eyes would glaze and they'd lower their voice – 'I could tell you a thing or two about Roy ...' – then they'd turn their heads and look round after they'd whispered their stories. It was always the same ... 'Don't tell Roy I told you.'

I had the feeling that if he'd walked through the door, they'd have jumped out of their boots. I began to hear stories about Roy that intrigued and astonished me. I didn't think that I could be shocked any more, but I discovered that Roy had a darker, more chilling side than I could ever have imagined. And the reverse was true; I heard about his kindness, his willingness to lend a hand to guys who were on their uppers and his work for charity ... he could be thoughtful, kind and considerate.

So had this wealthy entrepreneur with fire in his eye and a murderous background really mellowed? 'I'm a good boy now,' he says, in a voice that would melt marshmallows. And his violent profession? 'It's all in the past,' he told me with a barracuda smile. It's true that he's a millionaire, a high-level wheeler-dealer. But, although he smiles, his eyes are still as cold and expressionless as a pit viper. So who is the real Roy Shaw? What's he been up to since coming out of chokey? Is there a softer side to him? A woman in his life maybe? Are the chiller-killer stories true?

I wondered if Roy stills goes on the rampage even though now he has the financial clout not to bother? There's enough wealth and power rolling around him to hide a lot of sins and cover the bloodiest of tracks. Maybe he's mellowed, living the quiet life in his big house in the stockbroker belt and pottering about with his dogs in his garden? Somehow I didn't think so.

The crowds still melt away when he comes into a room. Tough, hard-bastard geezers get suddenly light on their feet and step out of his way when he walks across to the bar. Is it reputation? His awesome presence? Or do we put it down to animal instinct? Something we can sense, that Alpha Male, Leader of the Pack, Top Dog aura – he's the one who's going to lash out first and think afterwards, the man who has the fire in his belly to fight off all the others. Mr Nice or Mr Nasty? My gut feeling was that Roy Shaw was still as dangerous as ever.

I set off to drive to Roy's luxury home. Saint or sinner? I was about to find out.

CHAPTER 1

ONCE A FIGHTER,
ALWAYS A FIGHTER

I WAS LATE. It was a quarter-past ten and I had to be at Roy's for eleven-fifteen. I'd been feeding my ponies, Guv'nor and Geezer, and I'd lost track of time. I scrambled into my posh frock and ran a comb through my hair, no time to look in the mirror – Roy can't stand to be kept waiting. We'd been invited to Terry Spink's pub at Upton Park, West Ham. It was for the launch of Terry's new book. It was an important occasion and loads of the boxing world's greatest heroes were turning up to give their support.

The plan was that I was going to interview these famous men. I looked at my watch; it was going to take me an hour-and-a-half to get to Roy's and already my nerves were on edge.

I must have met every single hold-up between Sussex

and Essex – there were diversions on the Greenend Road because the council were cutting back bushes. There was a contraflow on the A271 where a gang of workmen were digging up the cat's eyes. And when I eventually made it to the M25, the traffic was shit.

At last I was in the leafy, upmarket stockbroker belt and pulled into the gravelled driveway of Roy's mansion. I even started to get out of the motor. I could see Roy coming towards me, his face was like chiselled granite, his fists clenched and there were two huge Rottweilers bounding along at his side. I didn't have to see their teeth – I jumped back inside and slammed the door shut. The dogs were jumping up and now I could see their teeth. Wow! I wound the window down the tiniest crack.

'Do the dogs remember me, Roy?' I yelled. It had been about a year since we'd last met. I'd been filming Roy for my *Hard Bastards* television series. The dogs are OK if you're properly introduced but how good were their powers of recall? Were they going to take time to reflect and weigh up the situation? Make a rational decision whether I was friend or foe? No way. They were barking their heads off and coming at me – it was open warfare. It was not the time for taking chances.

I was relieved when Roy snapped his fingers and called them off; they slunk behind him reluctantly but obediently followed him inside. I watched closely as he bolted the door and then came back to the car. Was he going to growl at me as well? But it was all right, he was in a good mood.

'Hi, Katie. How are you? Good to see you.'

Roy looked fit and sharp, his muscles solid under a light grey silk suit. Roy likes dressing well and looks the part in his Savile Row gear. He opened the passenger door and climbed into the front seat, leaning over to give me a peck on the cheek. He looked pointedly at his gold watch.

I took the hint and started the motor. 'We're on our way.'

Roy is now a successful businessman and property entrepreneur, but his reputation as an original hard bastard is unchallenged. He is still one of the toughest men in England today – a man who stands up for what he believes and never, never backs down. As we chatted on the drive back to London, I wondered what had made him like this.

'I suppose it was when I was a kid. I had to learn to fight, it was punch or be punched.'

'Were you bullied?'

'At school I was. There were four of them used to pick on me all the time. One day they collared me as I was going home. They were kicking and bashing me and I just got up. Something in me snapped, I'd had enough, and the adrenalin rush came right through me. I felt powerful. I didn't feel any fear. I waded into them and I done 'em. It was great. In that moment, when I saw them running away, I knew it was a gift. And then the same thing happened whenever anybody came up to do me again. Anyone who showed aggression to me, I would explode. That's the way things went on in my life.'

'You didn't take any nonsense from anybody?'

Roy shook his head. 'It worked against me when I was

in the nick. The screws would say, "Shaw! Over here!" and the adrenalin would come in and ... bang! I'd hit them. So that didn't work out quite so good.'

'For them and you both.'

Roy shrugged. That was the way it was.

There were still a lot of questions. What made Roy fire up like this? Why couldn't he ever back off? His expression had changed, become more thoughtful.

'What was your childhood like, Roy?'

'It was good until my dad died – that changed my whole life.'

'What happened?'

'He went out one evening on his motorbike and never came back.'

'Was it an accident?'

'A road crash. A lorry swerved out of control, and Dad lost control of his motorbike. He was killed instantly.'

'You never got over it?'

Roy shook his head. 'I was just a kid – one minute I was sitting in the garden with my dad, I was helping him, he was talking to me, kidding me about me wanting a dog, and going to the greyhound racing with him. My dad used to let me help clean his bike; we'd go down the garden to the shed and work away. He used to grow vegetables as well. I was always there, running round after him.

'We were best mates. Sometimes he took me out for a ride on the bike, on the pillion. There was nothing like it, going like the wind with me clinging on tight. Everything revolved around my dad in those days, he took me about with him, gave me little jobs to do, he made me laugh, kidding me about something or other.

'I should have been going with him that night; he'd promised to take me but one of his pals wanted to go, so he said it would be my turn next time. I felt real miserable but that's the way it goes.' Roy paused. 'If I'd been with him ... As it was, an hour later he was gone. I'd gone to bed. For some reason, I couldn't sleep. I heard a lot of noise downstairs and my mother wailing. I got up and looked through the banister rails – there were policemen and everyone was crying. I heard what they were saying but I couldn't really take it in. It didn't hit me 'til the day of the funeral. They'd bought me a new black coat. I hated it. And when I saw them lower my dad's coffin into the ground, it all came over me. I wanted to chuck myself in after him. That's when I knew I'd never see him again. My uncle had to drag me off. I went mental.' Roy blinked hard, after all these years, the emotion was still raw.

'It's a hard thing for a little child to face,' I murmured.

'I started screaming and hollering. My uncle took me home.' Roy turned his head away.

'You do a lot of work for children's charities ... does this have something to do with it?'

Roy brightened up. 'Yes. I try to put something back. Kids don't have any chance when things go wrong in their life. They can't sort it themselves – although maybe I did.'

'How do you mean?'

Roy tapped the steering wheel. The traffic had snarled to a halt again. It was going to be a close thing whether we'd get there in time for the start. We eased forward, stop, start, a few cars at a time. Roy went on.

'After my dad died, everybody was nice to me at home, but I had to go to school and the bullying still went on. Before, I'd always known my dad would stand up for me – but now I had nobody to back me up.'

'Why were you being bullied?'

'I don't know. It was just kids. There's always a victim.'

'And an aggressor.'

Roy smiled at me. 'Right. Anyway, when they cornered me, I knew I could run away, which was what they were expecting me to do, or I could stand and fight.'

'You took them on.'

'It came to me – that I didn't care about anything any more – after my dad had gone. I felt this load of anger inside me.'

'Because of your dad?'

'Yes. That gave me the rush of adrenalin through my whole body. They had their dads and mine had been taken away. It wasn't fair. I wanted to kill them. It was a strength I didn't know I had. A powerful feeling like nothing else on earth. All my anger and grief came out in those punches. I didn't feel any pain myself.'

'Were you getting hurt?'

Roy shrugged. 'I suppose I was. It didn't mean anything to me. It never does when I fight. It's as though I don't feel anything. What happens to me doesn't matter – the only thing is to beat the other guy, to knock him down, finish him. I have to win.'

17

'The eye of the tiger?'

'The same. I've always looked on it as a gift from God. I smashed those kids good and proper. They never came near me again. And that's when I realised that something can come out of even the worst pain. I was never going to be frightened of anybody or anything again.'

As I listened to Roy talking about his childhood, I thought that even his voice has an intensity about it. I had to lighten the mood – we were going into a room full of hyped-up boxers – one false move and it would be a row to end all rows.

We made it to the East End of London and eased our way through the traffic on the double-parked streets. It wasn't so far now. Roy began chatting about his property investments. He is a real charmer and great company. I learned about the houses he'd done up, his fabulous holidays, the cruises to the Caribbean and Far East. Roy is making up for lost time.

There was only one subject we didn't talk about – women.

I already knew that he had lots of girlfriends. This is a man who likes to party. So, I had to ask. 'Is there a lady in your life now?'

Roy shook his head.

'Come on. You've made it, you've got a fabulous house, a successful business, you've no money worries.'

'That's right, Katie.'

'So why do you live on your own?' I thought about him coming home to that big empty house.

'Being rich is terrific. I've done skint – I don't ever want to go there again.'

That wasn't quite what I was asking. 'There's no one to cook you a meal when you get in?'

Roy grinned. 'There's no hassle – I can please myself.'

'There isn't anyone special then?'

Roy was thoughtful for a moment or two. 'There was someone once ... who was very special.'

'Who was she?'

'A girl called Dorothy.' He kept his eyes fixed on the road, maybe so I couldn't see his expression.

'And did you love her?'

'She was the love of my life,' he told me simply.

I'd touched a nerve. There was a silence. I somehow knew that for the time being I mustn't go any further. This was yet another loose piece of the puzzle about this man who has more hidden depths than the Bering Straits. We were nearly there. I let it go. But I was going to ask him about Dorothy again, when the time was right. Who was she? And why had she had such a big impact on Roy? What had gone wrong?

We drove along Upton Park Road. The Rolls-Royces, Bentleys, Jaguars and Mercs were bumper to bumper. Damn. There was nowhere to park. We circled the pub a couple of times and eventually found a space opposite. Standing outside the pub was a bald-headed doorman, who looked a bit fierce and growling until he saw it was Roy, then he stopped immediately.

Roy pushed the swing doors open and we went inside.

I followed, feeling a bit apprehensive. What was I getting myself into? Britain's most violent gangster, a warrior with the tolerance level of a cornered rattlesnake and the last King of the Unlicensed Ring was about to socialise with the blokes on the other side of the fence – the legit licensed boxers. My heart was going thud, thud, thud – now I knew what it felt like going into the ring – 'Seconds out ...'!

CHAPTER 2

FINGER FIGHTING

IT WAS A PROPER EAST END PUB, NO FRILLS OR FANCIES OR WINE BAR PRETENSIONS – THERE WEREN'T EVEN CARPETS OR DECENT CURTAINS, JUST CURLING CIGAR SMOKE AND AN ATMOSPHERE YOU COULD CUT WITH A KNIFE. The place was packed, buzzing with noise and wall-to-wall with blokes past their prime, pot-bellied and flat-nosed pug-ugly. These guys were talking fast, huddled in groups, leaning on the bar and pressed up against the walls. They were drinking beer, bobbing and weaving, ducking and diving as they re-enacted their last fight, or the one before – even the boxing they'd seen on Sky the previous evening – 'If only ... ya should 'a' seen it ... he came at me with a right hook ... he went down for eight ... it oughta have been ...'

These blokes don't have blood in their veins – it's testosterone!

FINGER FIGHTING

My partner, Leo, is a boxer himself; even so, I felt a bit uncomfortable being there. These past-their-prime pugilists were still trying to win their fights – but now it was verbal sparring – each one of them was trying to outdo the other. It was all egos – World Champions, British Champions, Gold Medal Winners, Middleweight, Heavyweight – they were all there, the best of British Boxing – and the could-have-beens, the might-have-dones, all the boxing world's movers, shakers, fixers and hangers-on. They were all trying it on.

Living in the past most of them. I found it quite sad that these tough men were still reliving their fights, their glory days, their hard-luck stories – the fights they'd won and the fights they'd lost. They were still matching themselves with boxers they wished they'd fought ... or wished they hadn't.

I noticed that, as they were talking, their eyes were constantly darting round the room. There was an element of tension; I sensed they were waiting for something; an unspoken question was hanging in the air. The Pearly King and Queen were standing in the far corner – we were in for a knees-up and a rendition of 'Roll out the Barrel' and 'Show Me the Way to Go Home'. Was it to do with them? But why? I knew they were popular but these guys were on pins. I studied the crowd.

It took me a few minutes to figure it out. No, it wasn't the buttons they were looking at – it was the table next to them, it was loaded down with food. All eyes were focused on the lavish finger buffet – sandwiches, vol-au-vents, lots of plates covered in Bacofoil and underneath it were lots of goodies – cocktail sausages, ham, cheese and pineapple on little sticks and, best of all, spicy chicken wings. Mmmm.

The same question was on everyone's mind: when are we going to eat? But they'd have to wait, there were speeches first.

Roy was in no mood for socialising. He'd been out the night before and wanted to get this done and dusted. He pushed his way to the bar and ordered three glasses of sparkling water with lime juice and lots of ice and lemon. 'Right,' he said, rubbing his hands. 'Who do you want to interview first?'

As we sipped our drinks, a buzz went round the pub – 'Roy's in.' Within minutes, there was a seemingly endless stream of wide-shouldered blokes with noses as wide as double wardrobes, all coming up to shake hands and say hello.

Roy spoke to each one of them warmly and sincerely. 'Nice to see you, my old mate ...' and 'How are you doing, son?'

But he kept turning to me, his face blank. 'Who the hell was that?' All these people seemed to know him like a blood brother, but he didn't have a clue who most of them were. 'I've never been very good with names,' he hissed out of the side of his mouth. Even so, he was as polite as always, said a few words and wished them well.

At the far end of the room there was a long table and sitting behind it was Terry Spinks MBE, former British Heavyweight Champion.

Roy, Leo and I sat down near the front. I knew some of

the other geezers and Roy knew them all. 'That's Reg Gutteridge,' he whispered.

'The boxing commentator?' I asked.

Roy nodded. 'World famous.'

Next to him was Bob Lonkhurst from the Boxing Board of Control.

The speeches started, first one boxer then another came up to the front to have a few words and give their good wishes to the champ.

Looking at Terry, I could see that he wasn't in the best of health, but all these boxers, world champions and fellow sportsmen had turned up to give him their support. It was an emotional moment for him. One by one they went up and said their piece. I watched them and studied them carefully. Their words were eloquent and sincere but their eyes gave it away. What they were really interested in was the finger buffet.

The tributes and greetings were finally over. Roy started to get up.

'One more to go,' I told him. It was Bob Lonkhurst, the ghost-writer. He started his speech. At the start everyone was quiet, you could have heard a pin drop. Five minutes into it and there was a general shuffling – the boxers had returned their attention from the good words back to the Bacofoil.

These guys were getting desperate to know – was it really spicy chicken wings, or was it all cheese and pineapple? This was important, these guys are carnivores. They didn't want vegetarian. But Bob went on and on.

People began murmuring, 'How much longer?' A whisper went round, 'Is he reading the whole book?'

These are not the sort of geezers to sit through a lengthy speech. They do their talking with their fists, the universal language. Punching the hell out of each other is the form of communication they understand. Bob was still in full flow, but now nobody was listening.

Roy was sitting next to me like a rock. The finger buffet didn't hold the same appeal for him as it did for the others. He watches his diet and keeps in shape. No cholesterol. But the rest of the room was filled with an air of anticipation and trepidation. Was it meat under the silver wrapping or not? When could they start? Would there be enough to go round? At last somebody hissed, 'Shut the fuck up, Bob!' He looked a bit surprised but took the hint. 'Ladies and gentlemen, I believe there are some refreshments waiting' He gestured towards the very patient and still smiling Pearly King and Queen before going on, 'and in the right corner, weighing in at several hundred pounds, we have, courtesy of our generous host, a veritable feast of refreshments! Please help yourself to the finger buffet.'

There was a polite murmur of applause as cauliflower ears pricked up. Yeah! This was it! The Bacofoil was coming off! Chairs scraped on the floor as they were pushed back. Everyone shoved and muscled their way towards the tables. The suspense was over. Yes! Yes! Yes! It was juicy, spicy chicken.

It only took ten minutes and all that was left were

bones – strewn across the floor. I'd never seen men eat, fight and talk at the same time, but these blokes managed it. They were ducking and weaving and jabbing and bobbing even with their mouths full of chicken. I was trapped in the middle, doing a bit of dodging myself to scramble out of the way.

I had to get clear, there was chicken skin flying through the air, corned beef sandwiches clasped in meaty hands, slivers of pink ham dangling from mouth corners.

The atmosphere was filled with giant egos and testosterone. Each bloke was trying to get more, eat quicker, do better than the next. I made it back to where Roy was standing, well clear of the ruck. He looked at me and shook his head. It seemed as though the next fight was going to be over the finger buffet.

Eventually the table was empty and everything began to simmer down. They went back to talking about their fights, the winning, losing, the fame, the money, the good luck, bad luck and the hard work. I listened to them, it was all the same. They were all set on one thing – being the best. This was all that mattered to them.

I wondered if they'd have agreed to talk to me if Roy hadn't been present. I didn't think so.

I wanted to know what he thought about it all. 'Do you think these guys are a bit egotistical?' I asked.

'Sure,' he agreed. 'They all love the limelight.'

Roy was, as always, honest. I still couldn't understand why they were all so involved. 'These men are rich, they're already famous and successful, but here they are on a

Thursday afternoon, sitting in an East End pub, still talking about their glory days.'

Roy nodded. 'I can understand it. They're finding it hard to let go. When something's part of your life, like boxing, you can't give it up.'

I didn't think that many of them had even tried.

They were living as much of the same old lifestyle as they could, talking about boxing, thinking about boxing, going round to the gym, except instead of training they were fund-raising for this or that charity or talking about the book they'd just published.

'Do you think that boxing is just a job?' I asked Roy.

'No way. It's not something you can do nine to five. It's a hundred per cent way of life.'

'Yes. I can see that. It doesn't matter whether they're 16 or 60, does it?'

'They dedicate themselves to it totally. They never lose their will to win. It's grit and guts and determination.' Roy was jabbing as he spoke, his fingers pointing in the air.

I realised how much it meant to Roy, to all of them. What came across was that boxing isn't a job, it's not something you do nine to five, it's a way of life. Whatever their age, they dedicate themselves to it totally. They never lose their will to win.

When I met them at Terry Spinks's pub, that's what came across. Once they're hooked, boxing owns them. Once a fighter, always a fighter, that's what gets them to the top.

CHAPTER 3

ALAN KEEPS SCHTUM

I'D HEARD A LOT ABOUT ALAN MINTER – UK BOXING LEGEND, BORN 17 AUGUST 1951, WORLD MIDDLEWEIGHT TITLE, BRITISH MIDDLEWEIGHT TITLE, EUROPEAN MIDDLEWEIGHT TITLE – BUT WE'D NEVER MET BEFORE.

He'd agreed to talk about Roy while we were at the book launch at the pub. I thought that maybe he'd come across and introduce himself – 'Hello, Kate ... how are you ... nice day.' No chance. Alan is used to having things his way and, when I eventually caught his attention, he just nodded and pointed to an empty chair at his table. All right. No problem. I pushed my way through the crowd.

Alan was dressed for the occasion, a £500 navy-blue Crombie overcoat, whiter-than-white shirt, snazzy silk tie.

He looked every inch the retired World Champion boxer with a face like well-worn granite and he wasn't smiling.

As he greeted me, I noticed his hands. I couldn't help thinking about the damage those rock-hard knuckles had inflicted on human flesh.

I sat in the chair opposite; there were no preliminaries, we were straight into it.

'How long have you known Roy?'

Alan thought for a moment. 'I'd heard about him before I even saw him fight. In those days, all the up-and-coming boxers trained at the Thomas A'Beckett – it was in the Old Kent Road and everybody who was anybody or was going to be anybody came out of that gym. Roy was one of the youngsters to watch out for – he'd built up a reputation for himself.'

'What sort of reputation?'

'Right from the start we all knew he was a hard bloke – a man who gave out a lot of punishment. There were murmurs about his life outside.'

'Do you mean crime?'

'Let's say we knew he wasn't a man who took prisoners. When you get a man who doesn't know the meaning of fear or pain, it always builds up a following.'

'And that was Roy?'

Alan nodded. 'He was with one of the best trainers around, a man called Danny Holland. And the Thomas A'Beckett was the best gym in London. So he'd got himself well placed from the start. Danny wouldn't have taken him on unless there'd been a lot of potential.'

'What did you think of him as a fighter?'

Alan narrowed his eyes. 'Well, Roy had the killer instinct all right.'

'He still does!'

'I don't doubt it. I've been in his company. I know he's the business.'

'Did you see Roy socially?' These two out on the town was something to think about.

'We used to have a drink or two ... we liked going to a club in the West End – we'd generally finish up there. Winding down after we'd had a boxing do.'

'For the fight after the fight?'

Alan managed a weak smile. 'There's a buzz of adrenalin that takes a while to get out of your system. You're not feeling anything physical – the pain or anything. That's the next day. You're still revved up. You have to get it out of your body.'

'So it got a bit exciting at times?'

'You could say that. It didn't take much to set him off – but Roy could handle himself all right. I know the power of the man. When he set off, he was unstoppable. When he was going in, shit-all wouldn't make him change his mind. The man was and still is a right hard bastard.'

His words had a chilling effect. Coming from Alan, this was strong stuff. The man is no angel himself. In a fight in Italy, at the height of his career, his opponent died of the injuries he sustained.

He paused and took a sip of his drink, malt whisky and water. 'With Roy, once he started a ruck, it was personal. You knew he meant it.'

'What about his fights in the ring? Do you think he'd have made British Champion.'

Alan nodded. 'Without a doubt. Yes, he could have done it. There was no one to match him at the time. I don't know that there have been many to match him since. He was quick and he had a hell of a punch. A very strong man. And he had it written all over his face.'

'What?'

'It's hard to explain. Violence. Staring you down. Everybody backed off from him. There was something in his expression. You don't see it very often. But when you do ...' His words hung in the air.

'Stand clear?'

'Yes, that's it, Kate. You know what's coming and you don't want to go there.'

I saw Roy out of the corner of my eye, he was crossing to the bar and everybody was moving out of the way. He looked over to me and smiled and held up his glass. 'Want another drink?' he mouthed. I shook my head. Alan was looking round as though he was going to bite someone's head off. I tried to imagine what it was like when these two went out on the razzle.

'When you used to go clubbing, did you ever see Roy lose his rag?'

Alan shook his head. 'No. Roy's a gentleman. If someone took liberties, that was a different thing. He's not a man you'd want to cross. If you did, you'd be in trouble. I think most people accept that.'

'What about the bare-knuckle fights?'

Alan's face was without expression. He shrugged as though he didn't know what I was talking about.

'When he fought Lenny McLean?'

'Naw, I don't know anything about that.' He passed his empty glass to his gofer for a top up and pointed to my mineral water. I shook my head. Why was he being so evasive?

'Come on, Alan. I think you're giving me a load of bull now.' I was getting fed up with him pussy-footing around. 'Don't tell me you didn't know Lenny McLean.'

The whisky arrived and he took a careful sip. 'Yeah. Course I did. Lenny McLean ... the Guv'nor. He's dead now.'

'God rest his soul.'

Alan raised his glass. 'Amen to that.' He leaned forward and lowered his voice confidentially. 'I know more about Lenny than any man who's ever lived. Lenny used to drive me home when I was drunk. I used to have a good night out at the Hippodrome in London. Roy did as well. Lenny used to get me home. Drive me down to where I lived in Reigate.'

I was going to say 'that was every week then', but I looked again at his fists. No, I wasn't going to push my luck.

'What about the fight between Roy and Lenny?'

'It had been coming a long time. It had to happen. London wasn't big enough for both of them. They both had reputations. A following. Territory. You see, Roy had heard that Lenny was causing trouble for a pal of his – he had a pub in Hoxton.'

'What kind of trouble?'

'Lenny was a gangster. I don't know what he was doing to upset them but, anyway, Roy said he'd sort it. He went to the pub to have a word with Lenny. But he wasn't there and Roy couldn't find him.'

'So the word spread that he was looking for him?'

'That's right. At that time, when the name McLean crept up in conversation, people would say, "Hold on ... keep moving." He was a hard bastard and a fucking huge guy. He was awesome.'

'What did Roy do?'

'He laid the money on the table to have a bare-knuckle fight with him. It was an understanding that the winner took the lot.'

'And did Lenny agree?'

'Sure. He matched him. The venue was Sinatra's nightclub in Croydon and it was packed.'

'Did you go?'

'I couldn't have missed it. I think Roy had a bit of a shock when Lenny climbed into the ring. He'd never set eyes on him before. He was a fuckin' big bloke. They couldn't find a pair of gloves to fit him to start off – his hands were like meat plates.'

'And Roy?'

'There was no way he matched him for size but as for guts ... Roy only knew one way to fight – to win. He steamed into him straight away, hitting him in the body. Lenny was pretty confident to start with, he thought it was just another fight. He was calling out to the crowd, "Look, he can't hurt me."

'He didn't think it was going to be any trouble. There hadn't been anybody to match him. But all of a sudden he realised that Roy was different. Roy stuck him one on his chin and he felt it. Roy was a slugger, and he didn't know what it meant to lose.' Alan stood up suddenly, his fists jabbing the air. Bam! Bam! Bam!

I ducked back against the wall. Wow! Alan was still up for it, shadow boxing a ghost from the past. 'Roy went forward all the time, like this ... jabbing ... jabbing ... jabbing. Not letting up. He tracked him round the ring. It was savage. He kept up some heavy body punches. Smashing his ribs. Lenny was staggering. He was in agony. He was being crucified. Roy was still full of it. He'd got plenty left. He was tracking McLean like a hunted fox. But there was nowhere for him to go, Roy was all over him like a rash.' Alan was ducking and weaving, reliving his own fights through other men's stories. 'There was blood everywhere. Roy was swinging punches and Lenny was holding on to the ropes. You could see he'd had enough.'

But the past is one fight that no one can win and, as Lenny ran out of steam, Alan also sat down heavily.

'It must have been a bit of an upset.'

Alan shook his head. 'It might have rattled some. Maybe if they hadn't seen Roy fight before. But it was never in doubt. And definitely not after the first round. That was something else.'

'It was that violent?'

'Oh dear. Lenny was actually dripping blood. He was

having his face smashed to a pulp. The floor was slippery. Everybody knew that Roy wasn't going to let him go. It was like the gladiators in the Colosseum – the crowd were roaring their heads off. Lenny was groaning, he was doubled up. You could see he wanted to chuck it in.'

'So they finished it ?'

'No. They couldn't. Roy was still steaming. He was going on. There was no stopping him. He'd got himself psyched up for it and ... well, it was a massacre. They managed to get him off eventually. Roy would have kept at it until he'd finished him.'

'Do you mean killed him?'

Alan shrugged.

'So, you would say that Roy's a wild man when he gets going?'

'Roy Shaw is one of the most respected and looked-up-to men in London today. You'd have to be a fool to try to cross him. Or not have heard of him. He's one of the most dangerous men as well.'

I glanced across at Roy; he was chatting up a beautiful blonde young lady at the bar. He can be as soft as marshmallow when it suits.

'If he'd got his British boxing licence and gone professional, Roy thinks it would have made a hell of a difference to his life.'

Alan agreed. 'Without a doubt. He'd have had everything he wanted – legit.'

'If you could have matched him with anyone to make a top fight, who would it have been?'

There was no hesitation. 'Rocky Marciano.'

'Why?'

'Because they're the same. Powerful men. They weigh their opponent up and go to the finish.'

There was one question I had to ask. 'Alan, you were World Champion. Would you have fought Roy?'

He leaned back and thought for a moment, choosing his words carefully. 'You can ask him if he'd have fought me. But that's not a challenge,' he said in a flat voice.

I had one last question. 'You and Roy have moved in the same circles for a long time. You must have heard a lot of stories about him.'

Alan nodded. 'Without a doubt.'

'There must be something you know that not many other people do.'

His expression changed.

I went on anyway. 'Come on, Alan. I love secrets. Are you going to tell me a secret about Roy?'

The shutters came down straight away. Alan set his glass down and edged to get up.

'I don't know one,' he said. I was left in no doubt that the interview was over.

Roy was making his way across to us through the crush. He walked to the door with Alan and they looked at each other straight in the eyes. Then they shook hands and Alan Minter left without another word.

'How did that go?' Roy sauntered back, smiling. Friend or foe, he doesn't give a damn.

CHAPTER 4

BOXING CRAZY

ROY WAS ENJOYING HIMSELF. Admiring the view. Wherever you get powerful men and money, you get pretty girls and there were plenty at Terry Spinks's party.

'The brunette or the redhead?' I joked.

'I was thinking about the blonde,' he told me, nodding towards a young lady at the bar.

'A bit ...' I was going to say 'young' but then I saw his expression and thought better of it.

'Do you want to know what Alan said about you?' I asked.

'He told you I was a gentleman.'

He did as well. 'How did you know?'

Roy smiled.

'We were talking about how you got into boxing.'

'It was my dad's brother started me off. Uncle Alf. He took me to a boxing booth when I was 11. Up the Commercial

Road. We used to go to any boxing shows we could find. I knew even then that God had given me something.'

'Your fists?'

'Not just that. It was something else. Like a sort of strength. When I started fighting, I felt an adrenalin rush. An anger came over me like a red mist.'

'Does it still?'

'If I'm provoked,' he told me calmly. 'In those days, it was like a high-voltage current setting me alight. I couldn't feel anything – cuts, knocks, pain. It didn't matter if I got hit. It was an overwhelming urge to lash out. BANG! BANG! BANG!'

Roy's fists were clenched and his face was red. I took a step backwards.

'It was all my feelings coming out.'

'Was it to do with losing your dad so suddenly?'

Roy nodded. 'That was it. I wanted to hit back. I didn't know what I had in me to start with. But Uncle Alf saw it. And when I'd whacked my opponent and seen him cowering in front me, finished, it was like a primeval satisfaction. I can't explain it properly. I was trying to get my own back. Nobody was going to take anything away from me again. I wasn't going to be afraid of anything ... ever.'

'What about your first fight?'

'Uncle Alf took me to a circus tent. It was the Smith Brothers, they were putting on fights. He'd been trying to teach me, shadow boxing and tapping my face, that sort of thing.'

'Was he psyching you up?'

'He asked me if I was ready for it. I told him I was. But when it came to it, I felt a bit of nervousness. My opponent was a big lad and he'd fought before. He'd got all the proper kit, shorts and boots and a dressing gown.'

'What did you have?'

Roy laughed. 'I must have looked a sight. I'd got my sister's swimming costume as shorts. And I was wearing plimsolls. The gloves were miles too big. They weren't mine. The bloke before had been wearing them and they were sweaty.'

'You didn't have much of a chance.'

Roy smiled. 'That's what the kid I was fighting thought ... until I got going. He made a fatal mistake. He tapped me on my chin ...' Roy growled like one of his Rottweilers, '... it made me remember those bullies in the playground. It sparked me off – my anger was like a hot furnace inside of me, it was burning me up and I couldn't wait. It didn't matter about the gloves and the plimsolls. I went straight at him like a thunderbolt. The minute he came within reach, I let go with a big punch. CRACK! He went down on his arse like a sack of potatoes. The crowd went wild. Uncle Alf was jumping up and down. And I'd won £3!' Roy's face was shining. 'There's nothing better than a straight pound note, especially when you've won it fair and square.'

'You knew you were meant to be a boxer then?'

He nodded. 'There wasn't just Uncle Alf saw my potential. I started training seriously and boxing took over. It was my life. Before I was 16, I'd won the Area Championship and the Essex Championship and the Schoolboy Championship.'

'Glory days.'

'Yes.' Roy's face had softened.

Looking back, I wondered if he regretted that it had all gone so wrong. 'What did you think at that time? That boxing would be your career?'

'I was going to be World Champion. I was earning money doing what came to me naturally.'

'Fighting up and getting paid for it?'

Roy grinned. 'Something like that, Katie. I even fought the Old Bill one night.'

'One at a time, I hope.'

'My Uncle Alf took me to a police show. I remember to this day what he said to me before I went in the ring. "Knock his fucking head off!" '

'He didn't like the Old Bill?'

'He hated them.'

'Did you just do the boxing or did you go out to work?'

'My mother had got me a job at a machining works. I hated that factory. All I wanted to do was get out of there. It was full of mouthy, loud, gossipy factory girls. I'd rather have a slug-out in the ring than spend ten minutes with them.'

'Did you have a girlfriend?'

'Not then. I've had one or two later, though,' he told me slyly.

I had to laugh. Roy's womanising is legendary. Time to change the subject.

'I'd managed to get away from the factory and I found myself a job in a timber yard.'

'I bet that built your muscles up.'

'Chucking massive beams about ... it did. It was the best work I could have had. By the time I got my call-up papers, I was rock solid and I'd filled out. I was looking forward to the Army. I knew that the training would be tough but it would be good for me. They had boxing teams. That's what I set my sights on. I was 18 and full of myself. The fights and wins had given me confidence. I had muscles like iron and one hell of a punch. I was like dynamite waiting to go off.'

'Light the blue touch paper and stand back,' I murmured.

Roy smiled. 'Something like that.'

'So where did it all go wrong?'

Roy shrugged. 'I was anti-authority. All that ordering me about and telling me what to do. I thought the Army would be fair. I didn't realise that there are bullies in all walks of life. This was like the playground all over again. But this time I was up against the system.'

'And the system always wins.'

'Not always.'

'Why is that?'

'I just used to freeze and then ... whack!'

'What happened?'

'Well, I got the wrong side of the sergeant. He tipped my belongings on the floor because I hadn't made my bed right. I thought it was a liberty. I didn't like the way he talked to me.'

'You didn't know anything about the Army, did you?'

Roy laughed. 'Not a blind thing.'

'So you learned how to make beds?'

'No.

'I can't stand bullies and the sergeant was a bully.'

'You didn't hit him?

'I felt so raw and uncontrollable that there was nothing I could do. I couldn't have stopped it no matter how much I wanted to. I didn't want to. He didn't know what was coming 'til he hit the ground. Then it all went fairly quiet. The other soldiers stood looking at me with their mouths hanging open. One of them said, "Where did you learn to punch like that?" I told him, "Where I came from, life's like a dirt sandwich – the more dough you make, the less dirt you have to eat." And even by that time, I'd made plenty of dough. I wasn't going to eat dirt for anybody.'

'What did they do to you?'

Roy shook his head. 'You don't want to know.'

'Go on.'

'Nine months in the glasshouse. And it was brutal. They did everything at the double. I whacked another sergeant on the way in.'

'Why?'

'He was a nasty bit of work. Talking to me like a fucking kid, trying to humiliate me. I couldn't stop myself. I felt this explosion of anger inside me, the more I tried to keep it in, the more it was going to erupt. He asked me if I'd got it, like he was talking to a moron. "YEAH, I GOT IT," I screamed at him. And then *he* got it! I smashed him in the face, I felt his bones go crunch, he was like red jelly when I'd finished. They were pulling me off and I was still slamming into him.'

'How did they stop you?'

'Sheer numbers. Six of them all piled in and dragged me off.'

'One against six. You'd really blown it.'

An expression of sheer contempt crossed Roy's face. 'They dragged me bodily into a cell and then they held me down and beat me up one by one. They went on until they were too exhausted to punch me any more. I still tried to fight back, it was in my nature, but there were too many. Then they left me there. It was freezing and there were gaps under the door and holes. The wind howled all night.'

'Were you badly injured?'

'I suppose I was. But my body was like a rock; I'd been boxing and fighting and shifting timber ... I was young and strong. I was covered in bruises and cuts and I couldn't see out of my eyes there was so much dried blood.' Roy was silent for a moment. 'The next morning, they stripped me naked and dragged me outside.' He took a deep breath. 'It was the middle of winter and very cold. They took me into a yard and they'd got four officers with hosepipes ... they turned these jets of freezing water on me. It knocked me off my feet. I remember thinking that I couldn't breathe.

'And they were laughing at me. That did it. The fire was still in me and I rushed at the dirty bastards ... I was butt-naked but they weren't expecting me to have any fight left in me and I ran straight at one of them. I got the bastard holding the hose and managed to grapple him down on the ground and turned the hose round on the others ... they had a taste of it, I was blasting them with the icy water and they were squealing and yelling.'

'Were they shouting for help?'

'Yeah. A bit of icy water and they were like screaming little girls. They didn't expect it.'

'You're good at doing the unexpected.' I bit my lip. I'd heard people say he had the Devil in him when he was fighting.

Roy nodded. 'I like to catch my opponents unawares. I was gouging and punching everywhere I could. Their mates came to rescue them. You see, they thought they were tough nuts because they were in the Army and wearing a uniform. But they were nothing where I come from. I wasn't ever going to give in.'

'Did they keep you locked up?'

'It was a battle of wills. I had a cold shower every day.'

'With the hosepipe?'

'Yes. Until they realised ...'

'What?'

'That I would never, *never* give in. So *they* gave in. Seven days and I was back with the other prisoners. Although that wasn't much better. There were 14 of us in a unit; they wasn't a bad bunch of lads and I got chatting to another prisoner. They let us sit in a Nissen hut and have a smoke – one cigarette each – then they counted the stubs. Although I didn't smoke, it was just something to do. Anyway, this bloke started telling me about the boxing matches held between the units. He told me I ought to have a go. My aggression had been building up. It was the routine and the brutality. We were in the glasshouse, it wasn't necessary. But, like most experiences in life, it taught me something.'

'What was that?'

'Survival. At first I'd fought back but the staff sergeants were ruthless bastards. They'd seen it all before. So eventually I realised what a lot of other men in prison before me have learnt, that I could only beat them by surviving.'

'So you started boxing again?'

'When they realised that I could fight, they got me regular matches. The staff sergeant took a shine to me. Because it was always a good fight.'

'Did you win?'

'Yeah. I was his protégé. I was doing good, all the pent-up aggression I felt was let out in the ring. He was proud of me. I was his star. They were tough nuts from all over the country. All of them had been kicked out of their unit for one reason or another. They'd have been in prison if they hadn't been in the Army. They all thought they were tough, but to me they were big pussy cats. No problem. It offered me a way of releasing my aggression and doing the thing I loved best. Then my sentence ended and I was posted to Germany.'

'Don't tell me ...'

He nodded. 'Yeah. It all went wrong again.'

It seemed to me that Roy's life had been like a series of theme-park rides, terrific highs then loop the loop, and he'd be spinning wildly into another crashing low.

CHAPTER 5

WHERE THERE'S SMOKE, THERE'S FIRE

SAMMY MCCARTHY – BORN IN THE UK ON 5 SEPTEMBER 1931, BECAME A BOXER AND WON THE BRITISH FEATHERWEIGHT TITLE.

I knew that Sammy had known Roy for years; if anyone could tell me about the man inside the layers of myth and legend, it would be him.

Like a lot of hard men, he can be tricky to deal with. Whoever coined the phrase 'you can't judge a book by its cover' was talking about his guy. I didn't know what the hell I was getting myself into.

At the end of the interview, when I asked him if he knew a secret about Roy, I thought that all I'd get would be a stony look and a shake of the head. I couldn't have been more wrong. What Sammy whispered in my ear before he left had me gobsmacked. I'd heard some weird stories about Roy, but this one took some took beating!

Sammy came across as a charming bloke, smiling ear to ear, very friendly and pleasant – a cross between everybody's favourite uncle and Bagpuss. I sat down next to him; he was sipping malt whisky, wearing a Harris Tweed jacket, a moleskin shirt, discreet club tie and looking every inch the English country gentleman.

That's at first glance. Look a bit closer and *Watch with Mother* goes straight down the toilet. The smile doesn't ever reach his eyes.

Sammy shook my hand and asked me what I wanted to drink. There was a sparkling water and lime in front of me within 60 seconds.

I took a deep breath. 'You've known Roy a long time. How did you meet him?'

'How do you think? Fighting. He was always fighting. I first saw him in an amateur boxing booth. It was when he was just a kid.'

'What was he like?'

'Lethal. Even then. He was skinny but he was still knocking their heads off. He was maybe 18 or 19 when he really got going.'

'Is that when he was in his prime?'

Sammy shook his head. 'He hadn't even started. He could knock them out, though. He had one hell of a punch. And there was something else.'

'What was that?' I looked across the room; Roy had abandoned the young lady and was talking to Reg Gutteridge, the boxing commentator.

Sammy thought for a moment. 'It was something to do with how he felt. Rage or anger. Once he got going ... he liked it. Slugging them and seeing them go down.'

'Did he have a trainer?'

'Yes, Mickey Duff. He was well famous in those days. He'd seen Roy's talent and he took him on.'

'So, was Roy a good boxer?'

Sammy nodded. 'Yes. He was a strong fighter. A good fighter. He gave it one hundred per cent. The thing is, he was as strong as an ox, but not only that, he was nasty with it. That's what they could see in his eyes. He started off slugging it to 'em.' Sammy's fists were clenched, his hands up. 'Left hooks to the body, jabbing, an uppercut and that was it, they were finished.'

'Did he ever get hit?' Had Roy ever taken much punishment?

'It wouldn't have made any difference. Nothing that stopped him. Mind, it would have taken a ton of bricks to stop him. He gave it everything he had. And, so far as I know, he was never beaten. If he went down, he got up again. That was Roy.'

I knew from my own contact with Roy that he has a powerful presence. It says, 'Don't mess with me. You'll regret it.' I tried another tack. 'What about his reputation?'

Sammy's eyes narrowed. 'As a fighter?'

'No. Let's say, as a bad boy. You know about that?'

'Sure. Everybody knows Roy. He's a man who's made his own rules. He's never backed off from anybody. If they've been foolish enough to keep coming, then they've had to take the consequences.'

'And they were?'

Sammy shrugged. 'Roy always went on to the finish. Nobody shouldn't have messed with him.'

'You mean ...?'

He edged back in his seat. 'Yeah. Well, they all knew. If anyone fucked him about – they'd only do it the once.'

'Everybody knew this?'

'They had respect for him. A lot of respect.'

'Do they still?'

'Of course.' Sammy took a sip of his whisky. 'He's trod a hard road, has Roy. But he's paid his dues and come out on the right side.'

'A survivor, then?'

'Definitely.'

I wanted to know what Sammy thought about Roy's boxing prospects. What might have happened if he'd been allowed to continue his professional career.

'I saw Roy fight as a novice – you could see even then he was going a long way.'

'Did you ever see him get beat?'

Sammy shook his head. 'I think he had about ten pro fights under Mickey Duff. They were all wins and six knockouts.'

'Impressive. Did you know that the Boxing Board of Control took his licence away?'

He nodded. 'It broke his heart. He tried all ways to get it back. But he couldn't. They asked him what he'd been doing. I don't know what he told them but the people on the Board of Control are all QCs and within seconds they'd have known what the crack was. It was no go.'

'Why was that?'

Sammy gave me a hard stare. 'Maybe you should ask him that.' Sammy was sipping away at his malt and there was a bit of colour in his cheeks. I waited for him to go on ... I thought our talk was going well.

'His lifestyle got in the way. He was a bit of a Jack the Lad.'

I had to smile. 'That's one way of putting it.' I wanted him to open up a bit more. 'What was wrong with his way of life?'

'You couldn't have a life of crime and be a professional boxer. Roy wanted to have it all.'

'Do you think that it would have turned out different if he'd been given his licence back?'

'Yes, there's no doubt. He'd have given it all he'd got. Roy could easily have been British Champion. One of the things about Roy is that he was tough. He wouldn't give in. He couldn't be beat because he didn't know when he was beat.'

I wondered if Sammy had seen Roy's bare-knuckle fights. 'What did you think about his unlicensed fights?'

Sammy's face lit up. 'I've never seen anything like them since. I saw him fight a guy called Donny "The Bull" Adams. Have you heard of him?'

I nodded my head.

'Well, this man was called the King of the Gypsies – he was a vicious bare-knuckle fighter, a hard-faced mauler. I think Roy had come across him in prison. I knew they didn't like each other. The Bull was unbeaten, he'd had about 40 or 50 fights and won them all. He looked pretty confident – 'til it started.' Sammy grinned. 'It was a massacre. Roy had been training, he was as hard as nails. The Bull might have been fighting gypsies but he'd never met anybody like Roy. He looked as though he was going to kill him. There was no finesse, no grace. It was just violence. The crowd were hissing and spitting – they were there for The Bull. Roy was picking him up off the floor so he could hit him again. They had to drag him off. In the papers the next day it said PRETTY BOY TURNS UGLY. And that just about summed it up.'

'What did he win?'

'I heard that it was £3,000–4,000. He'd have had a bet or two. Not bad for half-an-hour's work.'

I realised that this was why people respected Roy. His fights, his whole life are the stuff of legends.

Sammy went on. 'I saw Roy beat Lenny McLean as well. Three rounds, that's all it took to finish him.'

'I'd heard as much.'

'Lenny was a giant ... as big as an ox. Nobody had ever beat him. I was amazed.'

'You weren't expecting him to win?'

'Nobody was. We had a pub and we'd organised a coach party to go down to see the fight, but I went in my own car. I had a Wolsley in those days.'

I looked down, hiding a smile. All these men love their motors and remember every one they've ever had.

Sammy went on. 'I was surprised at how well the fight was run. It was one to remember all right.'

'Did you see Roy's second fight with Lenny McLean?'

'No, I didn't, but I heard about it. They told me I'd missed a corker.'

'If you had to compare Roy with another boxer, who would it be?'

'I think it would have to be Rocky Marciano.'

Other boxers had said the same. 'Why is that?'

'It's for his enthusiasm. And he's quick and strong, like Roy.'

One of Sammy's friends came up and whispered in his ear and pointed towards the door.

I went on quickly. 'If you had to sum Roy up in one word, what would it be?'

'Respectful. Roy Shaw respects people, whoever they are and wherever they come from.'

'Have you ever seen the other side of him. Has he ever lost control when you've been out with him? Have things got out of hand?'

Sammy was emphatic. Whether it was true or not, he wasn't going to say anything wrong about his pal. 'No. Never. I've heard about it.'

'They say he'll give the Devil a run for his money when he loses his rag.'

Sammy moved his head slowly from side to side. 'I've never seen him do anything wrong.'

Roy certainly inspires loyalty.

Sammy had finished his drink and was rubbing his

hands together. I could take a hint; he was ready to go.

'Before you go, Sammy, there's just something else. Will you tell me one more thing about Roy?'

He paused. 'What do you want to know?'

'Tell me a secret.'

His face closed shut like a prison gate. He stood up. I'd shocked him. Grass up a pal? Never.

I took a chance and got up with him. I caught hold of his sleeve. 'No, not that, something else. Isn't there something about his private life?' I whispered. 'Come on, Sammy, have a think.'

He was deeply suspicious.

'I want to know something about Roy that you know and nobody else does.'

Sammy frowned for a moment or two, then suddenly he gave me a sly, mischievous glance. 'All right. I will tell you something. I don't know whether you'll believe it though.'

'What? Tell me, tell me.' Yippee! He'd given in. Sammy leaned forward. I was on pins. What was it?

'Maybe he'll tell you himself.'

'You tell me.'

'Ask him what his party trick is.'

I knew that Roy liked to go on the razzle. 'Is it that he can drink anyone under the table?' I'd been told that nobody could stay with him when he was in the mood to have a good time.

I followed Sammy to the door. He turned to me with a mischievous look on his face. 'No, it's not drinking.'

'What then? Women?'

'He likes the ladies, but it's something else – to do with his ...' Sammy cleared his throat ...

WHAT! Had I heard him right? I felt my face go blood red.

'I've not seen it myself, thank God,' Sammy added, giving me a sly Cheshire cat grin.

'You wanted me to tell you ... now you know. Why don't you ask him?'

I shook my head. No way. No way.

He disappeared into the crowded street and, for once, I couldn't think of anything to say.

CHAPTER 6

IT'S DO OR DIE

'WHAT'S HE BEEN TELLING YOU, KATE?' I turned round to find Roy standing right behind me. Those steely-blue, dead shark's eyes are set above a nose like corrugated iron. Roy has an unnervingly hostile expression and he was staring straight at me. Was he reading my soul?

A shiver went down my spine; it's hard to know what he's thinking. His unpredictability is part of the danger – there is no justification for Roy's violent nature. Anything can trigger it off, although he's always been the perfect gentleman towards me.

I began to wonder if talking about him to his pals was such a good idea. If he'd heard what Sammy had been saying, he was keeping schtum.

'Where's your lady friend?' I asked.

He looked across the room. 'Gabbing to her mates,' he replied.

I needed to get him to lighten up or this was going nowhere. 'Are you taking her out later on?'

His face cracked into a big smile. His eyes twinkle and he looks totally different when he's thinking about something good. 'Yes. For a drink, maybe a bit of supper at Langan's. Maybe a club later on.'

I shook my head. Where did he get his energy from? I hoped she could keep up with him.

'When I was talking to Sammy...' I hesitated. What the hell ... 'He was telling me about when you lost your licence to fight.'

Roy's face hardened. 'It set my future for me. The Establishment decided I wasn't going to be a boxer.'

'Why was that?'

Roy lifted his shoulders. 'I'd been in too many scraps.'

'Scraps?'

'You know. I'd been using a different name – Roy West. That was what I called myself. I thought I might get away with it, but I suppose that, in my heart of hearts, I knew it was a slim chance.'

'Had you been in prison?'

'Once or twice. I had to go to see the British Boxing Board of Control. It was like an interview. They knew the boxing was all right. But they were solicitors and QCs and top-brass policemen.'

'Not a lot of chance of keeping any secrets then?'

'No. I told them a few porkies but they weren't having any of it. They decided my destiny for me. I got a letter in the post. "Roy Shaw, you cannot have a licence to box." It was like a punch in the gut. One of the worst days of my life. Boxing was all I lived for, it was what I knew. I could have made it – and kept on the straight and narrow.'

'There's nothing like a straight pound note ...'

'That's right. But I didn't see many of them. There was only one road left to me when they turned me down.'

'And where was that?'

'Villainy.' Roy grinned. 'What had I got to lose? I was as mad as hell. They'd taken the one thing I wanted to do away from me. I made my mind up that I was going to be a villain.'

Roy pushed through the crowd and found us a space near the empty tables. We sat down. Now he wanted to talk.

'Had you been in trouble with the law before?' I asked him.

'Just a bit.' I noticed his fists were clenched. 'When you're a career criminal, it goes with the territory.'

I looked at him expectantly. It's an unwritten rule – don't ask about what they call 'business'. If he wanted to tell me, he would do. Roy took a long drink of his mineral water.

'I was already on the run from Borstal when all this was going on – and, just my luck, I got picked up on Christmas Eve. You see, I was out with my mates and there was a bit of a fight. We were at the Ilford Palais, and I knew one of the bouncers – it was another boxer – Billy Walker ...'

'The Blonde Bomber?'

'Yes. British Champion. Billy had watched a few of my fights, he knew what I could do. They'd got a bunch of lads in from Canning Town. "The big five" they were called. Trouble-makers and real nasty with it. Billy asked me to give him a hand.'

'So you politely declined and said you'd another engagement and went on home,' I teased.

'Yeah ... well, maybe that's what I should have done. Instead, I waded in and it turned into a free-for-all. Broken bones, bloody heads, the works. I was punching away and the next thing I knew the riot squad had come and I was on my way to Cardiff Prison. Don't ask me why.

'But anyway, there were two of the "chaps" there already and they were right cocky Londoners – the Welsh hated them. When I turned up, I was the third cocky bastard. I was fighting from the word go.

'Eventually, I went to court and I got three years for bashing a doctor and escaping from Borstal. I finished up in Wormwood Scrubs.'

'How long were you there?'

'Not long. I went on to Lewes Prison in Sussex.'

'You moved about a bit.'

'None of them could handle me, that's why. I'd had a row with a fella in the gym, called McCulloch. He was built like an ox and he thought he was top dog and he could push anybody around. It didn't work with me.

'He came at me and I stopped dead in front of him. He thought it was a joke. "What's the fucking matter with you?" he asked me. He found out when I hit him smack in the jaw. I heard the bone crunch – it was a cracking blow. He was pole-axed.'

I winced as Roy smacked one fist against the other palm

while he was telling me this. His hands still looked like lumps of iron.

'I'd caught him completely by surprise. He just lay there moaning. I stepped over his body and walked away.'

'End of story?' I asked.

Roy shook his head. 'Only the beginning. McCulloch had to go into hospital, his jaw was smashed and I had to go in front of the Governor. He told me he was sending me to a man's prison in a man's world ... before I knew what was happening, I was handcuffed in the back of a prison van again and on my way to Maidstone.'

'Did you settle down there?'

Roy gave me a quizzical look. 'I settled them down. It was all all right 'til we got drunk one Christmas.'

'Drunk? How did you manage that?' Prisoners are not allowed any alcohol.

'Blame the Catholic Church.' Roy smirked. 'There was a pantomime and everyone was involved with it. The joke is – it was *Ali Baba and the Forty Thieves*! They'd got a few more than 40! Me and a couple of mates were backstage boys – helping to move the scenery – and one of them was a model prisoner and a staunch church-goer. He'd managed to pinch a couple of bottles of Communion wine, so we had a little party of our own – down amongst the cardboard camels.'

'Did you get caught?'

Roy shook his head. 'Not at the time. It wasn't until I went back to my cell later on that the booze hit me. One of the screws must have noticed my legs buckling and he called the prison doc. I asked him what the fuck he wanted. I was going to offer him a drink but I'd drunk it all. I thought it was real funny.'

'But they didn't?'

'No sense of humour. One of the screws punched me in the guts and I stopped laughing. It wasn't funny any more. "You shouldn't have done that," I told him.'

I knew what was coming next. 'You lost it big style?'

'And some.' Roy shook his head. 'I grabbed him and nutted him in the face. It went from bad to worse. I could only think, who the hell does he fucking think he is? I was screaming and hollering at him. They legged it out and locked me in the cell. I told them they would be sorry because, when I got out, hell was coming with me.

'I was smashing the door, I couldn't stop myself, it was like the adrenalin rush when I'm fighting. I hit the door with the chair and actually caved the metal in. By the time I broke the door in, the screws had all gone, they were nowhere to be seen.

'The prison was in a riot, the other cons were screaming their heads off – encouraging me and yelling with delight that I'd got out. One of my pals asked me what was up and I told him I'd just ripped the fucking door off my cell. He had a look out of his window and he saw the screws preparing to storm the wing – riot gear, truncheons, dogs – the works. He pleaded with me to give myself up.'

'Did they come on the wing after you?'

Roy grinned. 'It was a farce. They ran towards me. I ran at them brandishing my weapon.'

'Which was?'

'A chair leg! And they all ran away. It was complete mayhem.' Roy paused, looking reflective. 'I gave up in the end. They fetched the Governor. We had a chat. I did a couple of weeks in the block and then they shipped me off to Canterbury Prison. This is what it was like.'

I nodded. 'You didn't really expect to get your boxing licence, did you?' I asked him.

Roy shook his head. 'No. It was a dream. It meant everything to me, but it was never to be.'

'How long were you in Canterbury?'

'Not long. They shipped me almost straight away to Pentonville. Whilst I was there, I met three of the most feared men in the system – Mad Frankie Fraser, Jimmy Andrews and Jimmy Essex.'

I'd heard of them. Who hasn't? But they weren't physically big men like Roy. 'Why were they feared?' I asked.

'Because if you were foolish enough to fuck with them, you knew without a doubt that they'd be be back to cut your throat. I got into so much trouble with these geezers that at one stage it was stamped on my prison records: "SHAW AND FRASER MUST NEVER BE IN THE SAME PRISON EVER AGAIN." '

Roy began scanning the room, looking for his new lady love. He saw her chatting to one of the minders and he was across the room like a rocket.

I noticed a man heading towards me; he pulled out the empty chair.

'Do you mind if I join you?' he asked.

CHAPTER 7

THE LAST KING OF THE UNLICENSED RING

I'D DISCOVERED THAT ROY SHAW is a complex character. He fights to the death. He chucks strangers over balconies. And yet this self-styled Guv'nor of London's underworld works hard for charities, looks after his old mum, loves his dogs, is a romantic at heart and is still pining for a long-lost girlfriend.

He admits to having a temper from hell but ask around – the word on the street is that he's a great guy, a magnificent human being, a legend, a phenomenon, a boxing idol. There's no doubt that he commands the ultimate in respect.

It's hard to figure out how these two personalities can be rolled into one. This whole thing was becoming a mass of contradictions. I hadn't a clue what I was going to find out next.

Roy had wandered off to look for the blonde babe. The party was starting to wind down, the food had gone and some of the guys were looking a bit the worse for wear.

'Do you mind if I join you, Kate?' someone said, approaching my table. He shook my hand.

'Be my guest, Reg,' I replied as he sat down.

I looked into the smiling face of Reg Gutteridge, the famous boxing commentator. He was looking suave and sophisticated, crisp shirt, cashmere overcoat and every inch the world-renowned fight-game analyst. Reg comes from a fighting family and is perhaps the best-known boxing reporter throughout Britain and Europe. He is also an inductee of the International Boxing Hall of Fame – he knows the fight game inside out, upside down. If anyone could tell me about Roy's career, it would be Reg.

Reg had enjoyed meeting up with his old chums; he was mellow and keen to talk.

'You've known Roy a long time, is that right?'

Reg smiled. 'Yes. We go back a long way. I used to train alongside him at the Port of London Gym in the East India Dock.'

'What can you tell me about him?' I asked. 'Does he live up to his reputation?'

Reg nodded. 'And some. But I'll tell you this, Kate, Roy has always been well liked and respected all over the East End.'

'What about his boxing?'

'Impressive. I saw him fight as a novice at Mile End Arena. He won every time.'

'Was he a good fighter?'

'Sure. Roy has always been a hard man. He could fight. A hard slugger. He had the same style as Marciano, that was the way he fought, coming in throwing punches from all angles. It gutted him when he lost his licence.'

I'd heard the same from all these men – 'If only Roy had kept his licence ...' What did Reg think about this? 'Do you think he should have been allowed to fight legit?'

Reg thought hard. 'Why did he lose his licence?'

I guessed he probably knew the answer, but I told him anyway. 'Well, he was a bit of a naughty boy in those days.'

'A criminal?'

'Yes.' There was no other way to put it.

'What I think about it is this ... If I was on the Board of Control, I would have had to ask myself – can I condone this? I can understand their actions to a degree, but on the other hand, you've got to give a man a chance. There's more villains in striped trousers and carrying briefcases than there are out on the streets. I hate them more than anyone. They're hypocrites. I can handle the hard men like Roy, they don't mind taking their stick now and then.'

I agreed with Reg. 'What about Roy's style of fighting – do you think he could have been British Champion?'

There was no hesitation. 'Yes. But, because of the life he led, it wasn't to be. Very rarely does it happen.'

'That criminals become boxers?'

'The criminal world and boxing have always gone hand in hand. I don't know why this is particularly. Although footballers have done time for fixing matches, it seems to be different where boxers are concerned. Boxers have a reputation for being hard and the media don't want to see a poof being a boxer.'

I thought about my ex-husband. 'Ronnie was.'

'Yeah, yeah.' Reg nodded. 'I wouldn't have said that to his face though.'

I felt sad for a moment. 'Ronnie was always such a good friend to me.'

Reg had a slightly cynical expression. 'Generally speaking, genuine criminals have never been good fighters. Now Roy is a fighter first and foremost. He's like Tyson – he's another man that could fight before he got into trouble.'

'Do you think there are comparisons?'

'Undoubtedly. With Roy it was crime. But with Tyson it's all about women.'

I thought that might be oversimplifying it a bit, but I could see where he was coming from.

'Times have changed now,' Reg went on. 'It might all have been different for him these days. Roy had a lot of staying power. He fought an American boxer called Ron Stander when he was in his late thirties – I think he'd come out of prison – and the next thing he had this fight. They all said he'd be past it at that age. Stander had been fighting top-class, he'd been matched with Joe Frazier a year or two before.'

'What happened?'

'Roy went in there and just about slaughtered him. You'll have to ask him to tell you about it. There were boxing promoters from all over the world there. America, Germany – they all wanted him to go and fight abroad.

'He wasn't even a licensed boxer and he'd proved himself better than some of the professional heavyweights.'

'That must have meant a lot to him.'

'Undoubtedly. It was a sort of victory over boxing's ruling authorities. They'd tried to ban the contest.'

'Why was that?'

'They considered it medically unsafe. They had a man of 39 boxing outside of the rules. Ron Stander was ten years younger than Roy, he was world ranked, he'd been fighting former World Champions.'

'So Roy's first battle was to be allowed to fight.'

'Yes, they wanted to ban him altogether.'

'How did he get round it?'

'Roy did the fight for charity. For the disabled kids. And people wanted the fight to go ahead. He proved himself to the lot of them.'

'It was a good fight?'

'Roy hammered him. It only went three rounds. Stander retired with two broken ribs.'

'Wow!'

'The offers poured in after that.'

'Didn't he take them up?'

Reg shook his head. 'No, I think he'd done what he set out to do.'

'What was that?'

'Prove himself. He wanted to show everyone that he

was world class and that's what he did. He could have been World Champion but at that time circumstances were against him.' Reg looked up, his driver was standing by the door.

There were a couple more things I wanted to ask him. 'If you had to sum Roy up, in one sentence, what would you say?'

Reg didn't have to think about it. 'A hard man and I would not want to tangle with him.' He stood up. 'Look, you've someone else waiting to talk to you.' He pointed towards the bar. Bob Lonkhurst was edging our way. 'I'd better leave you to it.' Reg stood up, ready to leave.

'One last question,' I asked.

'Go on then.' He turned back. 'What is it?'

'What about telling me a secret ... there must be something you know about Roy that nobody else does.'

That made him stop in his tracks. 'There could be ...' I could see that he was weighing it up. He smiled suddenly. 'Yeah. I've got a little titbit for you. I've told you he's as hard as nails – but that's not always. Did you know he looks after his mother?'

I shook my head. No I didn't.

'He's like a lamb with her. He thinks the world of her. She's getting on and not so well now – there's nothing he wouldn't do for her. He even does all her shopping ... you wouldn't think he had it in him, would you?'

Reg pulled up the collar of his expensive coat and gave me a quick peck on the cheek. A whiff of cigar smoke and expensive aftershave and he was gone. I didn't even have time to thank him for the interview. I wasn't really surprised by what he'd told me about Roy at the end. I guessed that there was an emotional core inside the fighting man. It was good to know that I wasn't the only one to see a different side to Roy Shaw.

CHAPTER 8

ACHY-BREAKY HEART

'WOULD YOU LIKE ANOTHER DRINK?'

As Reg left, Roy materialised suddenly by my side. I have always found him to be the perfect gent, a man of sharp contrasts, smiling and charming even though he might be telling you the most horrific real-life story. He was full of smiles when he came back from the bar carrying a sparkling mineral water for himself and a lime and lemon for me. 'What do you think?' he asked, nodding towards the young blonde lovely who was teetering away from the bar and in the direction of the Ladies. I chose my words carefully. Mentioning her age was an obvious no-no – she looked all of 21. And I wasn't going to make any comment on her dress sense – a bare midriff, 'fcuk' skimpy t-shirt, denim mini and those 6in Jimmy Choo stilettos! I prayed she wouldn't drop anything on the floor – if she bent down to pick anything up these guys would forget all about the finger food – there'd be a riot!

Roy had a reputation for liking the ladies and this one was 'sex in the city' eat your heart out. But what I said was, 'She looks very nice ... I think you've pulled!' I nodded. He was like a kid in a candy store. I didn't want to deflate his ego but ... he was in a good mood, maybe now was the time to find out about his love life. 'Don't you ever want a permanent relationship, Roy?' I asked in a matter-of-fact tone.

'What do you mean?' He frowned.

'Marriage. A partner. To feel a close bond with another human being. Somebody being there for you when you come home.'

'I've got my Rottweilers.' He grinned at me. 'They're always pleased to see me. And they don't say, "Where you been? ... What you been doing? ... Who've you been with?" '

'There is that,' I agreed. 'But they don't cook you a meal, either.'

Roy shrugged, brushing a stray blonde hair from his sleeve. 'I like to eat out.' 'What about when you're ill? Colds, 'flu?'

'I don't get ill,' he growled.

'All right. When you want to talk to somebody.'

'I'll ring you up, Katie.'

I gave up. Roy always has to win. Was that the problem?

Roy looked down at his hands, they are square and strong with big knuckles. 'I know what you mean, though,' he said quietly. 'I've tried being married ... It didn't work out.'

I'd seen pictures of Roy's first wife, she was a stunner. 'Why was that?'

'We were happy, but ...' He shrugged. 'Too much came between us.'

'Like what? Other women?'

Roy shook his head. 'No. It was prison. That's what finished it. She would have stuck by me. She was waiting for me, we loved each other. If it hadn't been for the stress of visiting ...' His voice trailed off. 'It was the way I felt inside,' he said quietly. 'The way I behaved. I couldn't help it.'

'What went wrong?'

'I was away for too long. I was jealous. I'd be picking over her letters, looking for a hidden meaning, trying to find something that wasn't there. Prison does your head in. Even for an average man. You're locked up 23 hours a day, there's nothing to do.' 'Except think.'

Roy nodded. 'That's the trouble. Every minute seems like an hour, every hour seems like a day, a week's like a month, a month's like a year. It's hard to realise what it's like for the people you've left on the outside – their life is going on, they're going out, they're meeting their friends, everything's carrying on. You have to accept this, they're cut up but they are managing without you.'

'And that's difficult to come to terms with?'

'Impossible. You've too much time to think about it. When she came to see me, I'd have been looking forward to it for weeks. I was living for seeing her walk through that door – the first minute I'd blow it.'

'What did you do?'

'I'd have all the right things ready to say but something would always set me off. If she was happy, I'd wonder why. If she looked miserable, I'd think it was guilt. If she'd made an effort, had her hair done, put some make-up on, nice clothes, I couldn't believe it was for me. Was she meeting someone else? I'm locked up in here and she's seeing some bloke. It's like a poison gnawing away at you. You've got to have a visit or else she'll think you don't want to see her. But the visit is agony. They fetch you from your cell and you're waiting to go into the visiting room. You're thinking, Has she come? What if she's forgot? If she doesn't want to come? If she's got something bad to tell you?'

'An emotional see-saw,' I murmured. I've visited my husband in prison. It's a bitter-sweet experience. I could tell by Roy's face that he was reliving the pain.

'Even if the visit was all right, it would be hell when she left. Watching her walk out of the door and I couldn't go with her. It churned me up for days.'

'You found it hard to trust her.'

'At that point in my life, I couldn't trust anybody. I couldn't trust myself half the time. I used to think about how much I loved her. She was on my mind day and night. That's how it is for men in prison. There's always someone they fixate on. Blokes in prison fall in love very easily.' Roy took a long drink of his water.

I'd heard this before. 'Maybe it's a form of escape?'

Roy nodded. 'I'm sure. When she used to come to see me, my stomach flipped.'

'Was it a whirlwind romance?'

'Not at all. It was an old-fashioned courtship. I knew she was the one from the first time we met. Her family were strict, though, and I had to win her trust. I courted her.'

I could imagine Roy liking to do that, wining and dining her.

'She was pure and childlike. Very naïve. That's what I liked about her.'

'Everybody else you knew was just the opposite?'

'That's it. I wanted to give her everything. In a way, that led to more trouble for me.'

'How come?'

'When I first knew her, I'd just come out of Pentonville. I was short of readies, so I had to find some work.'

'Driving a bus? That sort of thing?'

Roy laughed. 'Proper work, that didn't entail eight 'til four-thirty and hard graft.'

'Villainy?'

Roy raised his hands, palms upwards. 'What else did I know how to do? They wouldn't let me box ... I'd no trade. I wasn't going on the dole queue. Villainy. It was all I knew. I'd got in with a nice little firm who were doing blags. Factories and local firms on pay-day.'

'Robbing them?'

'It couldn't have been easier. We found out the wage routine first off.'

'How did you do that?'

'We watched the banks. Stood outside and clocked who was going in. The same faces arrived the same day every week. Getting the cash out and putting it in their cars and driving back to the office. It was a piece of cake. And we were a team. It was worked out like a precision operation.

'Every man had his own role, each as important as the next. We had a lookout for the Old Bill and an anchor man – to make sure everyone got away. The rest of them were in the ramming car ... one we'd pinched earlier. It was to stop the target no matter what it took.'

'So you crashed it into the car with the wages in it?'

'That's right. Then Albie would jump out and open the boot. He was a genius at it, he could open any boot in seconds.'

'You wouldn't have time to ask them for the key?'

Roy gave me a sideways glance. I couldn't help but think it was like something out of an American gangster movie.

'What did *you* do?' I asked him.

'I was the heavy,' he told me. 'I was there for the violence. I'd dish out whatever was necessary.'

I shivered.

He saw my expression. 'Nobody got hurt. So long as they did what they were told.'

'I shouldn't think they had much option.'

'It was all prearranged,' he went on. 'I'd be standing on a street corner waiting for the car to come past. When it approached, I'd roll down my balaclava and run out into the road and throw a house brick straight through the car window.'

'Wow! That's a shock for anybody.'

'That was the idea. They always slammed the brakes on. They didn't know what had hit them. And the ramming car would slam into them. They weren't going anywhere. I'd run up and shout at them, "FUCKING SIT STILL! DON'T FUCKING MOVE!" They used to cower like little mice.'

I could imagine that. 'Were you armed?' I asked hesitantly.

'Didn't need to be,' he told me. 'I carried an Indian club. That was enough. I'd swing it round a bit, bash the car door, threaten them. Albie would have the money in his sticky paws and we'd be away. The poor unsuspecting workers wouldn't know what had hit them.' He paused. 'It wasn't as though it was their money.'

'Their wages,' I reminded him.

'The firms were always insured.'

'You heartless so and so,' I told him.

Roy smirked. 'We were good at the blags. We used to go all over doing them. It was a good time for me. I was riding high. I'd got a good few quid in my pocket and the beautiful girl, who I adored, was waiting at home for me. We'd been married in Malta. It was pretty damn good. I thought it would last for ever. I thought we'd be together for the rest of our lives,' he mused.

'Wasn't there any chance of you getting back together when you came out of prison?'

Roy pulled a face. 'I went round to see her but it was

never going to happen. We were already finished. She'd cheated on me while I was inside.'

'It must have been hard for her, ten years away?'

'That wasn't the point. It was hard for me. She'd enjoyed the good times. She had a boyfriend while I was inside, but I got that stopped.'

I'd heard the rumours. I didn't know whether this was a road I wanted to go down. But there no holding him back. 'I had a prison visit with your Ron.'

'Ronnie?'

Roy nodded. 'At that time, I was away and I couldn't sort things myself. He did me a favour.'

Oh. I felt goose bumps. 'What sort of ...' The words wouldn't come out. I knew these men's reputations. I wished I hadn't asked. Roy went on, talking casually. This was no big deal. But now I had to know. 'The favour Ronnie did ... What happened to the man ... was it ...?'

'Oh yeah.' Roy's eyes had narrowed. '*Bad,*' he told me with chilling intensity.

I felt suddenly cold. These are not men anyone should mess with. Roy looked directly at me. Was he gauging my reaction? The room was still buzzing with people but it seemed less cheerful and friendly. I looked around, the smiles were sinister, the eyes watchful, all the faces hiding dark secrets. 'No regrets, then, Roy?' I asked hesitantly.

He shook his head slowly. 'To regret is to be sorry and I'm not sorry for anything – he got what he deserved.'

Roy wasn't giving that another thought. He was mulling over his relationship with his wife. 'You can't put the clock back,' he said slowly. 'I knew that. We both might have wanted it, but there was no chance. It was my kids I wanted to see most of all. They're my flesh and blood. I wanted to feel their loving embrace. They were only little and I'd missed them. I didn't know what to expect. What she'd told them. I couldn't help wondering how they were going to react to me.'

Roy has close family ties. His kin are of supreme importance to him. 'But it was all right?'

His face cracked into a big smile. The blue eyes lit up. 'It was fantastic. My daughter Chatina ran straight up to me as soon as she saw me. She threw herself into my arms and smothered me with kisses. "Daddy! Daddy! Daddy!" she squealed. I could feel the tears streaming down my face.'

'What about your little boy?'

'Gary? He stood his ground, eyeing me up, a bit wary. He's a chip off the old block all right.'

'But he came round?'

'Yes.'

'And are you still close?'

'Yeah. They're terrific.'

'And your wife?'

Roy shook his head. 'No way. On that day, I was just out of prison but there was no chance of a talk. Nothing like that. We could have sorted a lot out between us. But she'd got her boyfriend there. The door was open and I could hear them talking. I slipped in the flat quietly. He was telling her he loved her and that he wanted to stay with her.'

Oh no. I knew what was coming.

'This is what I had to listen to after ten years inside. I walked straight in. My wife saw me. I could see the panic in her eyes. "Roy ... how ... when ...?" I knew she was pleading with me. But I was too angry to say anything. Then the boyfriend stepped towards the door. He hadn't a clue. But my wife knew what was coming. She saw the look on my face and she let out a scream. I rushed forward and picked him up bodily. The red mist was flooding through me, it took over totally. I don't know how much he weighed, he wasn't a small bloke, but I ran with him, up the hallway, through the front door and on to the landing. I felt an indescribable rage and I chucked him straight over the balcony.'

I saw that Roy was clenching and unclenching his fists. His face was livid. 'What did you do then?' I asked him quietly.

'I put my hands on the concrete rail and leaned over and looked down at him. He was lying on the concrete. Very still. He was face down and his leg was folded under him, unnaturally. There was a pool of claret flowing into the gutter.'

'What did you think?' Maybe this time Roy would have realised he'd gone too far?

'I felt better. I remember thinking it was the best place for him.'

Why did I think it could be any different? 'So that was the end of your marriage?'

'It had been finished a long time before, but that totalled it,' Roy agreed.

'Hasn't there been anyone else since?'

Roy took a deep breath. 'Yes ... and no.'

'Come on. You'll have to tell me now.'

'I've been with some lovely ladies over the years.'

'That's not what I'm wanting to know. Has there been anyone special?'

His face was serious now. 'Yes. Dorothy ...'

I waited for him to go on.

'She was my first love ... and only love,' he whispered.

'So why didn't you two stay together?' I asked.

'Because I blew it. She wouldn't forgive and we split up. It was crazy because she meant the world to me. There's never been anyone like her. After all these years ... I still think about her. A lot.' Roy is full of surprises.

'Do you still see her?'

He shook his head. 'No. I haven't seen her for years.'

'Where does she live?'

'That's the problem. I don't know. I did see her a couple of years ago. But we hardly said a word.'

'Where was that?'

'I was filling my car up with petrol. I was at a motorway service station, near Debden. I'd been to a charity boxing match the night before. I was on my way home, not thinking about anything when, all of a sudden, a girl came up and pinched my bum.'

I burst out laughing. Roy grinned. 'Yeah. I couldn't believe it, either. I looked round and there was Dorothy. I was gobsmacked!'

'What did you say?'

Roy Shaw – ready for action.

Donny 'The Bull' Adams – one round.

Terry Hollingsworth – one round.

Starbuck – one round.

Three world-class fighters – Jack O'Hallaghan, Terry Downs and Ron Stander – with Roy and his boy Gary.

'Our prices can't be beat – just like Roy Shaw.' One of Roy's advertising campaigns.

In the COUNTY OF HERTFORD

Petty Sessional Division of HERTFORD and WARE

To   Roy SHAW

of   ~~Unknown address~~   PORTERS AVENUE, DAGENHAM.

Complaint
~~Information~~ has this day been [~~or was on the~~
~~12~~] laid before me, the undersigned Justice of the
Peace by   Inspector Wardrop
of   Hertfordshire Constabulary
for that you, on the   19th   day of   October,   1975,
at   Wormley West End   in the County aforesaid,

intend to take part in a prize fight and it is asked that you the said
Roy SHAW be bound over to keep the peace.

Against the Peace.

You are therefore hereby summoned to appear on MONDAY
~~Saturday~~ ~~Thursday~~ the
~~20th~~ 20TH. day of   October,   1975, at the hour of
TEN in the forenoon, before the **Magistrates Court** sitting at the SHIRE HALL,
HERTFORD, to answer to the said Information.

Dated the   13th   day of   October,   1975.

ALL COMMUNICATIONS SHOULD BE
ADDRESSED TO:—

THE CLERK TO THE JUSTICES,
BAYLEY HALL,
HERTFORD. SG14 1EL.

TELEPHONE NO: HERTFORD 4242
EXTENSION 428/430.

Justice of the Peace for the County aforesaid.

One of Roy's many summons …

Roy's Rottweilers – Castor (*top*) and Rocky (*bottom*).

'I couldn't say anything – it caught me totally off balance. I was so stunned, I couldn't react. She'd already filled up, she'd gone in to pay. I just kept on filling up my motor. I wanted to speak to her and I was trying to hurry up. But nothing seemed to work, I was putting the hose back in the pump and trying to get the petrol cap back on. I was thinking what I was going to say to her when she ran out and jumped in her car and off she went.'

'She never came to talk to you?'

'Nothing. She looked great as well. Nice car.'

'You did get the number plate?'

He shook his head. 'I told you, Katie, it caught me on the hop. I've been trying to find her ever since.'

'What have you done?'

'Everything I could think of. I've asked all her friends. It's a wall of silence.'

Hmm. Did this mean that Dorothy didn't want to be found?

Roy went on. 'I've been back to where she used to live. Her last address. I've even put ads in the papers.'

This was more serious than I'd thought – 'DOROTHY, PLEASE GET IN TOUCH, I MISS YOU.' Roy a romantic? Was it for real? Or is Roy a man who only wants what he can't have? This was all news to me; at last I was getting a glimpse of deep and intense feelings. Was this Roy Shaw's secret? One or two of his pals might have suspected there was something about Dorothy, but had I discovered the soft centre that no one else knew about? Roy looked so down and miserable that I had an urge to do something to help him. 'Look, Roy, I know people who're good at this sort of thing, researchers and journalists – they're good at ferreting things out. What if I try to find Dorothy for you?'

His eyes lit up. 'Would you do that, Katie?'

'I'll give it my best shot,' I told him confidently. 'Leave it to me, I'll find her for you.'

Roy was looking at me as intently as a shipwrecked mariner who's watching out for a sail on the horizon. He's not a man who takes disappointment easily.

I bit my lip. Find Dorothy? I hoped to hell I could.

CHAPTER 9

BAD BOYS

BOB LONKHURST HAS KNOWN ROY FOR OVER 20 YEARS. He is technically on the other side of the fence – he's an Inspector for the Boxing Board of Control, and a boxing historian. So was he responsible for sending Roy back into the unlicensed fight game wilderness?

'No, but I think it was inevitable,' he told me. 'Everyone knew Roy could have been British Champion, but when you've been in a ruck with the Old Bill then you've had it. It was always going to be hard, if not impossible, to get back into it. He knew the rules.'

I'd walked over to the bar with Bob; he bought me a glass of sparkling mineral water.

'He was gutted by it, though,' I murmured.

Bob agreed. 'I think they're a bit more lenient now. There's always been favouritism in boxing, though. It isn't right. If you've served your time and paid your dues, that should be it. '

'He'd have had more chance now?'

Bob nodded. 'I don't doubt it.'

'Does boxing always go hand in hand with tough guys?' It seemed to me that boxers are a certain stamp of men. 'Are they always bad boys?'

'It's a way of channelling their aggression. If it wasn't got rid of, they'd get into trouble. Boxing saves you. Some young lads are mad – if they take up boxing, it saves them.'

'Have you ever seen Roy lose his rag?'

Bob was cagey. 'Well, you don't want to be around when he does that. He wouldn't do anything without a reason. But if he has a reason – stand clear. I saw him have a terrible fight outside a nightclub – I'll never forget it. There was some argument about whether he should be allowed in or not.'

'Where was that?'

'It was a newish club, a bit upmarket, in Romford. I think Roy enjoyed going there ... I went once or twice and it was all right.'

'Cigars and champagne?'

Bob smiled. 'Chatting about old times, people we knew. Course, Roy usually had a young lady on his arm.'

'That figures. So what went wrong?'

'Nothing. To start with, there was no trouble, no incidents, nothing. I called round a week or two later and all hell let loose. Roy was barred. He'd turned up with his girlfriend and they stopped him going in.'

'I can imagine how that went down.'

'The week before it had been "Come in, Mr Shaw, pleased to see you, sir," giving him the VIP treatment. The next time he goes, it's "Get the fuck out of here." '

'Why was that?'

Bob pulled a face. 'The police had paid them a visit. The past never goes away. Someone was stirring it and the bouncers had been told to give him grief.'

'They must have been brave men.'

Bob drummed his fingers on the table. 'Foolish. Roy tried to be reasonable, he asked to see the owner, but you could see he didn't like being mugged off.'

'No, he wouldn't, especially when he was with a lady.'

'He'd not caused any trouble; in fact, he'd been treated as a celebrity. I think what pissed him off most was that no one had bothered to have a word with him.'

'Maybe they were scared?'

'Maybe. But you couldn't just send a couple of bouncers to tell him to go home. He'd been doing the job before they were weaned. Anyway, the owner wasn't coming out and you could see that the bouncers were feeling as though they could handle the situation. They were psyched up, pumping their muscles, strutting like turkey cocks. There were three or four of them, all big guys.'

'Safety in numbers.'

'That's what they thought. I saw Roy tell his lady friend to go and sit in the cab. He still looked as cool as a cucumber, but I knew straight away what was coming. He was seething inside. It was just like watching a volcano erupt.'

'What happened?'

Bob's eyes widened. 'They hadn't a clue. Roy walked up to the nearest one – the guy had a blank look on his face, he didn't know he was in trouble. I think he thought Roy was going to have a word.'

'And did he?'

'Not a chance. He slammed into him with a punch like a sledgehammer! The geezer went straight down and stayed there. Roy had gone mental – he stood his ground in front of them, pounding his fists, his face was red and his eyes were blazing. He'd got his mouth open in a grimace and I swear he was snarling like a grizzly bear.'

'It was the red mist.' Roy had told me that when he was angry a sort of rage came over him, he couldn't control it – maybe he didn't want to control it. It was an adrenalin rush too powerful to halt.

Bob went on. 'The bouncers were too chicken-hearted to face him one to one. They all jumped him together. The biggest of them hit him over the head. His skull went crack! It staggered him, but he straightened up again and went forward, almost without any effort. It was enough to floor a normal geezer.'

'Roy's told me he doesn't feel any pain when he's fighting.'

Bob nodded. 'That must be true. It was like watching a wild animal. No matter what they did to him, they couldn't stop him. He was gouging their eyes, they were screaming and yelling, there was blood everywhere. I think they all realised together that they couldn't hold him. They'd have had to kill him to finish it.'

'So what did they do?'

'Roy fought them back inside. One after the other escaped into the club until they were all in. And they locked the doors. He was as mad as hell.'

'Did he leave it there?'

Bob gave me a quizzical look. 'Roy, leave it? I doubt it. He was still yelling when I drove off. He invented "I'll be back" before the Terminator.'

I looked across the room. Roy was at the centre of a small group of men and women; they were all talking and smiling and he looked happy and relaxed.

'Do you think people act differently around him?'

'It's inevitable. Even if they don't know his reputation ...' His voice trailed off. Bob paused for a moment. 'There's something about him, an inner strength, without thinking about it you know he's somehow dangerous, that he won't give in, no matter what.'

'So, if you were to sum him up in one sentence, what would you say?'

'That Roy Shaw is a nice man.'

Very diplomatic, but after watching a row like that, who could blame him?

'Would you say he's a good man who sometimes does bad things?'

'He gets carried away a bit.' Bob smiled. 'Let's leave it at that.'

Bob Lonkhurst is a nice man himself and totally immersed in the world of boxing with all its varied and larger-than-life characters.

I looked round at the nearly empty room. The air was fuzzy and stale with smoke and broken promises. It was grubby now, the floor littered with cigar stubs, trodden-in crisps and paper-thin dreams that had been brought out of their boxes, dusted down and relived briefly. The bright, fleeting buzz of enthusiasm and glory was gone 'til the next time. The party was over. Roy was shaking hands, saying goodbyes.

I walked with Bob to the door, wondering if anyone but me felt the sadness. All these blokes were brave and, whether good or bad, they had been physically strong and fearless champions. But boxing is a sport of youth, only the memories last. And that's where men who are fighters first and foremost differ – it's in their blood. They fight 'til they die.

I couldn't wait to be out in the fresh air, but I had one last question for Bob. 'If you knew a secret about Roy, would you tell me?'

Bob shook his head. 'No.'

'Isn't there anything, something most people don't know? His personal life maybe?'

Bob glanced at Roy who was saying a last fond farewell to the blonde. It looked as though she was writing her phone number down for him and they were arranging to meet again.

'He's got a way with women, that's for sure,' Bob murmured. 'But I will tell you one thing ... maybe it's a secret, I don't think many people know it, I don't know whether Roy would admit it even.'

'About his love life?'

Bob nodded. 'All these different girlfriends. He's always looking for someone. I once heard something about there being a girl he really fell for, but she ran away, left him. Maybe that's a secret. He's got a broken heart.'

Bob slipped quietly away as Roy came up and took my arm. 'I'll drive you back home, Katie,' he said. 'Good party. What did they all have to say about me?' He was still bouncing as he walked me, like the perfect gentleman he always is, to the motor.

If only you knew, I thought to myself.

CHAPTER 10

SHOCK TREATMENT

THE DRIVE BACK TO ESSEX WAS UNEVENTFUL. Roy was quiet, deep in his thoughts. I tried to get the conversation going.

'What was the fight like with Ron Stander?'

Roy shrugged. 'I won in three. Broke his ribs.'

That was it. I tried again. 'What about the row outside the nightclub?'

'I sorted it.'

'What about revenge?'

'What do you think, Katie?'

For the moment, he wasn't saying. I started talking about his audacious robberies, the long prison sentences, the fights inside. Roy wasn't having it.

'All a long time ago.'

I asked him about his mum. 'How is she?'

The blue eyes flashed. 'I'll take you to see her one day.'

'I'd like that,' I told him. 'The girl you were talking to seemed nice. Are you seeing her again?'

He shook his head. 'I dunno.'

Roy obviously had something else on his mind. When he clams up, nothing will get him talking, so I gave up and dropped him off at his door.

He paused at the electric gates at the end of his driveway and turned, looking at me directly. 'Have you found Dorothy yet?' he asked. Ah, now we were getting to it.

'Shouldn't take long,' I told him more confidently than I felt.

He lifted his hand in a wave and went inside, closing the door quietly behind him. A millionaire in an empty mansion.

I hoped that I would be able to find her. And soon.

* * *

I'd asked Roy if he'd come down to see me at the pub my partner Leo and I had bought. It's in Kent, the garden of England, and it's a lovely place. Ye Olde Yew Tree Inn dates back to the Middle Ages and it's full of oak beams, stone-flagged floors and steeped in history.

Village tales have it that it was the haunt of smugglers, with brandy kegs in the cellars and secret cupboards to hide from the Excise men. I hoped that Roy would fall for the cosy ambience, log fires, a well-stocked bar and a smashing Olde English restaurant. Our chef Tim is one of the best chefs in the county.

I made Roy's mouth water when I rang him. 'Prime steak cooked in brandy sauce, Yorkshire puds, sticky toffee pudding.' It was all fresh, home-cooked food.

Roy's mouth was watering and he arrived just before lunch and we wined and dined him straight away. Leo, Roy and I went to have our coffee in the snug. My dogs took to him immediately and lay down at his feet as though they'd always known him. They say that dogs are a good judge of character and, if that is so, then Roy is solid gold. Our mutts adored him.

I started asking him when his life started going down the tubes. 'When

did it all start to go wrong, Roy?'

He settled down in his chair and sipped his espresso. 'When I went in the Army, I suppose. That's when I realised how much I hated authority. I couldn't cope with it. I survived the glasshouse, then I got straight into bother in Germany.'

'What happened?'

He gave a short laugh. 'In retrospect, it was bound to happen. They sent me out to lick the enemy – it was a military manoeuvre. A raid on Dutch soldiers. We were in a convoy of lorries and then my vehicle was pulled out. I was supposed to stay put, on lookout duty. It was boring after a while and I fell asleep. The next thing I knew there was all hell breaking loose. Terrific loud noises, firecrackers and bangers, explosions going off all over the place. It was supposed to be like real warfare. I was half asleep, I thought, Fuck me, it's for real. I thought we really were being attacked.'

'What did you do?'

'I jumped out of the lorry and got myself into a ditch. I crawled on my belly to see what was happening. I thought if I put my head up I was going to get shot. I did what the Army had taught me to do. Get back to my regiment.

'It was like hell, guns firing, bombs going off. I suppose that was the point of it, to get us used to warfare. It was mayhem everywhere. Blokes running about with guns and yelling and nobody seemed to know what was going off.

'I was trying to get out of there and I crawled through a hedge. The trouble was, either I was going the wrong direction or they were – I landed right in the middle of a party of Dutch soliders.'

'The enemy?'

Roy nodded. 'Yeah. What with the noise and everything, I forgot it was an exercise. I couldn't help myself, it was instinctive, them or me. I smashed one with my rifle butt, then I took out a second. They were yelling at me, "NO! NO!" It didn't do any good. I'd lost all sense of reality. I was a real solider in a real war. And I was going to kill the enemy and escape.'

'And did you?'

'I nearly killed them. And when I made it back to my regiment, I was still full of it. I stumbled into camp shouting about the Dutch soldiers in the woods.'

'I bet that went down well.'

Roy gave a rueful smile. 'Yeah, well. They all limped into camp as I was telling the tale. Broken noses, broken ribs. They looked a mess. I looked at them and knew I was in the shit.'

'It was a mistake, though.'

'The Army doesn't allow for mistakes. If it had been a real war, I'd have got a medal. But what I did get was to be confined to barracks pending a court martial.'

'Did they let you off in the end?'

Roy looked sheepish. 'Mmm. They might have done, except ...'

'Oh no. Don't tell me. What could go wrong if you were grounded?'

'I got fed up with it. My mate Jimmy used to go to a dance hall and one night I got fed up stopping in by myself. So I found a conveniently open latrine window and went on the town myself.'

'You didn't get back safely before morning, did you?'

Roy shook his head. 'I would have, but ... we got involved with two girls, right lookers they were. But we couldn't speak German and they couldn't speak English and somehow they got pissed off with us. They do things differently over there. If you want to dance you have to put your name on their list. But we didn't know that. Anyway, the two girls were going to have a go at Jimmy, one of them rolled her sleeves up, ready for a punch-up. I couldn't stop laughing. It would still have been all right, but two of the doormen came over. They thought it was trouble, but actually it was only a bit of fun.'

'You got mad?'

'No, actually I didn't. I just wanted to have a dance,

have a few beers and then get back before anyone noticed. I think Jimmy had supped more than a few before I got there. He was in a nasty mood. He told the doormen to fuck off. I kept telling him to leave it out. They were polite as well. They didn't want any trouble. But he wasn't having any of it. They tried to get him to leave but he held a bottle up and called one of them a "Kraut bastard".'

'It was all over for you then.'

'Yes, Katie, that did it. I knew it was going to go off. I whispered to Jimmy out of the corner of my mouth that I was going to take the biggest one. He was like a bulldozer, with muscles like steel and hands like big meat plates. His face looked as though it was carved out of rock. I thought to myself, Fuck it, I'm never going to top him. I didn't know what I was doing there. It was the last thing I wanted.'

'Did you get hurt?'

'Katie ...' Roy gave me a reproachful look. 'In a split-second, I weighed the situation up. I knew I'd only have one shot at him – a punch was no good, it wouldn't even rock him. I had to catch him right and throw all my weight behind it. I clenched my fist, twisted my body and hurled myself at him. I hit him with a left – I felt him stagger and I followed it with an uppercut. He wobbled and fell over like a big old tree that's been hit by lightning.'

'Didn't anybody try to stop you?'

Roy shook his head. 'They were falling over themselves trying to get out of the way. Jimmy looked at me and I looked at him. We were both thinking the same. Let's get the fuck out of here. The dance floor parted like the Red Sea to let us through. Even then it would have been all right. We would have got away with it.'

'But ...'

'Yes, there's always a but. The doors to the street were glass. Jimmy pushed his and it swung open. I pushed mine but it was bolted. My fist went straight through the stained glass.'

I shuddered. 'I bet that hurt.'

Roy showed me a thick white scar across his knuckles. 'No. Not at the time. It bled a lot, though. We ran like mad things, trying to put as much distance from the dance hall as we could. Eventually, we came to some narrow streets and a quiet district and we found a seedy little bar on the outskirts of town. We went in and ordered a couple of drinks. I was trying to keep my hand under the table so it wouldn't be seen.'

'Did you get caught?'

Roy nodded. 'The German Police are thorough. All they had to do was look for two Englishmen – one with a cut hand. They got round to the bar eventually. When they came in I told them I was a mechanic and I'd cut my hand on a machine.'

'Did they believe you?'

'We didn't wait to find out. I hissed to Jim, as soon as they get us outside, we're having it away on our toes. They frogmarched us to the door and, as soon as we were outside, we ran for it.'

'In different directions?' I asked.

Roy was animated. 'Yeah. I don't know what happened to Jim, but I ran like the blazes. The Germans were yelling after us: "STOP, YOU ENGLISH BASTARDS."'

'And did you?'

'They were firing at us. I thought, What a fucking cheek, we won the war! What am I running for?'

'Everything had gone horribly wrong.'

'That's what happened. One thing after another. I never meant it to turn out like it did.'

'So did you get into trouble?'

'I kept thinking it couldn't get any worse and then it did. They sent me in front of the Commanding Officer the next morning. He told me I was the scum of the earth.'

'How did you take that?'

'I jumped over the table and head-butted him. The Regimental Police hauled me away. I think they wanted to string me up there and then. But next morning, one of the guards came to have a talk to me. I thought he'd got it in for me but he was trying to do me a favour. He told me he recognised himself in me. That I was anti-authority. I knew that already. He said that I'd be going away for a long time and that there was only one chance of getting away with it. I had to pretend that I was mad. Tell them that I was hearing voices. Then they'd send me to a mental hospital and I'd be shipped back to Britain.'

'It sounds a bit dramatic.'

'That's putting it mildly, Katie.' Roy hunched down in his chair. I fetched him another coffee and put a splash of brandy in it. These were painful memories.

'They had me in the nut house so fast it made my head spin. The next thing I knew, I was having ECT – electric shock treatment. I didn't know what I was in for at first. One of the doctors and a couple of male nurses took me down a long corridor and into a ward with rows of beds on either side. There were men in all the beds, lying there staring vacantly in front of them. They were like zombies. I still hadn't got it. I kept asking them what the fuck was happening. They put me on a table and four men came from nowhere and strapped me down. I was getting nervous and kept asking them what they were doing but they didn't answer. They were just smiling like evil vipers. It was all in a day's work to them, they didn't give a fuck. One of them pushed a big piece of rubber into my mouth, it tasted foul and made me gag. I thought I was going to choke. I felt my heart pounding against my rib cage, I couldn't move, it was a terrible feeling of absolute panic. One of the men wet my forehead and then I felt a searing pain in my head, as though my brain was being fried. I know that my body arched and then ... I must have lost consciousness.

'The next thing I remember is when I was lying in one of the beds in the ward, with the sheets pulled up to my chin. Looking like one of the other lost souls, I guess.' Roy stared into the fire. I didn't know what to say to him.

'They did that to me eight times,' he told me quietly. 'After that first time, when I knew what was coming, it took eight of them to hold me down.'

'How did it make you feel afterwards?'

'It was torture. A load of bollocks. Didn't make any difference to how I felt about anything. But the German doctor came to see me and told me that I was cured. My brain cells were in the right place at last and I'd be OK. They shipped me back to England, to a mental asylum.'

'How did you get out of there?'

'I was given a dishonourable discharge for being mad and they just let me go. I went back to my mum's, back to a hot dinner every day, a comfy bed and the realisation that, if I wanted any money, I'd have to either get a job on a building site, working in the mud and the rain or ...'

'Settle for a life of crime?'

Roy gave a manic laugh. 'No choice was it, Katie?'

CHAPTER 11

WHO'S A NAUGHTY BOY?

I DIDN'T KNOW WHETHER ROY WOULD STAY FOR THE REST OF THE DAY OR NOT, BUT I PERSUADED HIM TO TAKE THE DOGS FOR A WALK AND HE ENJOYED IT. Our pub backs on to a superb nature reserve, a wetland area with swans and lots of wildlife. It's just the place to blow bad thoughts away.

Roy came back looking fit and happy. The dogs were wrecks, covered in mud and completely worn out.

I made a pot of tea and Roy sat down at the kitchen table. He seemed completely at ease, so I decided to ask him about his life of crime.

'Were you always in trouble? When you left school, did you get into petty crime, then progress to ...' I paused; it was hard to know how to phrase it. Proper villainy? Being a full-time gangster?

Roy shook his head. 'It wasn't like that. I could earn money boxing.'

'It had to be worth your while?'

'I was Jack the Lad.' He grinned. 'Nice suits, respect, plenty of dosh to throw around.'

'So how did it all get started?'

Roy leaned forward. 'My sister's boyfriend got me into it. Terry, he was called. He was a flash git, expensive clothes, clean hands, always plenty of money. But he never seemed to have a job.'

'Did you wonder about it?'

'Yes, but I didn't suss him out straight away. He was waiting for her in our front room one night. She took forever to get ready. And he was always looking in the mirror. Combing his hair. Fancied himself, I reckon. Anyway, this time he turned round to me and asked me if I liked his suit.'

'And did you?'

'You bet. It was blue with a velvet collar. It was all the rage – Teddy Boy gear.' Roy leaned back in his chair. 'He asked me if I wanted a suit like his. I thought he was mugging me off. 'Til he told me how I could get one.'

'He was involved in crime?'

Roy nodded. 'He was a right little tea leaf. He started talking about a robbery he was planning. Course, it wasn't just conversation. And it wasn't anything to do with suits. He needed me on the team. He wanted a heavy. Terry was ambitious but he couldn't do the violence.'

'He wanted you to be a partner?'

'Yeah. It was to rob a bookie. It sounded easy enough. He'd been watching this bloke. He'd found out all about the cash he was stashing away to evade the tax man. We were going to relieve him of it. That was the idea.'

'So you went along with this?'

'Yeah. It seemed better than working on a building site. We weren't taking it from anyone who couldn't afford it. I've never throughout my life done that.'

Roy, like many other gangsters I've known, follows a strict code – you don't hurt women or children, you don't rob anyone who's poor. Not exactly Robin Hood, but it's better than nothing.

'That's how it was. And Terry convinced me that it was easy money.'

'This was the first robbery you ever did?'

'Yeah.' Roy began tapping his fingers together. 'We were right little amateurs. Talk about planning – we didn't even have gloves or balaclavas. But it was a doddle anyway.'

'What happened?'

'Terry had already sussed out what time the bookie left on a Saturday afternoon. It's a good time to do anything, half the world and most of the coppers are at the football match. Anyway, we watched him come out of the office and then we followed him to where he lived. It wasn't hard to keep track of him, he had a big Jaguar car. He pulled into his drive and parked up in front of the door. We sat across the road in Terry's car and we saw him lean into the back and grab a big holdall.'

'That was the money.'

'Yeah, loadsadosh. I'd felt a bit iffy about it before, I couldn't believe it was going to happen. But that psyched us up. When he went in the house, we waited a minute or two and then walked up the drive and knocked on the door. It was as simple as that.' Roy looked up at the ceiling. I waited for him to go on.

'Nothing happened and we knocked again. We were feeling anxious, fidgety. Somebody was saying, "Come on, come on." And then the door opened slightly. Smash! We shoved it wide open and barged straight in. There was only one thing we weren't expecting.'

'What was that?' I asked.

'There was a woman there. Terry hadn't bothered to find out whether the bookie was married.'

'Was it his wife?'

'Yes and there was a kid. They were frozen to the spot; the little lad was clinging on to her. They didn't know what was happening. The bookie did, though, straight away. We tied him up to a chair and he was pleading all the time for us not to hurt his wife and son. He was irritating me. What sort of an animal did he think I was? I'd never hurt a woman or a child. I told them to go in the next room out of the way. And then I asked him about the money. Where was it?'

'Did he tell you?'

Roy stared down at his hands. 'He was a stupid fucking bastard.'

I took that as a no.

'He kept saying there wasn't any. I wasn't having any of

113

it. I told him there were two ways we could do it – the easy way or the hard way. But whichever – I'm walking out of here with the money. And I gave him a little tap. It probably broke his nose. It made it bleed anyway.' Roy shrugged. 'He wasn't thinking straight. He could see I meant business. He was tied to a chair, his family were in the next room and he was telling me that there wasn't any fucking money.' Roy clenched his fists.

'He made me angry. I set about him. Where's the money? Bang! Where is it? Bang! There was blood all over his nice carpet. Bang! It didn't take more than a minute or two – but he could have saved himself all that.'

'He told you?'

'He was begging to tell me – he was screaming it.'

'Where was it?' I said.

'You're not going to believe this, Katie. It was in the biscuit tin in the cupboard. All £3,000 of it.'

'Did you split it with the others?'

Roy nodded. 'We had a grand apiece. I thought I'd got it made. I told my mum to pack up work and I bought my sisters a record player. I went and fitted myself out with the flash suit and blue suede shoes. It felt good.'

'How long did the money last?'

'Not long enough. We hadn't a clue how to be professional about it, we were flashing it around. It wasn't long before the Old Bill were on to us. The next thing I knew, I'd been arrested, convicted and sentenced and I was on my way to a cell.' Roy shrugged. 'If you can't do the time, don't do the crime.'

I'd heard cons say this before, it's like a prison mantra. They don't have an option though, do they?

I poured Roy another cup of tea. 'Didn't it put you off crime, though?'

Locking a young man up away from his family in the harsh prison regime is to protect the public but, if Roy is anything to go by, prison is no deterrent.

'It only made me determined to plan better. They wouldn't catch me next time,' he replied with a sparkle in his eye.

'You're a proper rogue,' I told him. Roy looked at his watch.

'Do you have to go?' I asked. There was a lot more I wanted to know.

'I thought it might be teatime,' he told me, rubbing his hands.

The chef brought in a plateful of ham and mustard sandwiches and salad and pickles.

Roy has a tremendous appetite for all the good things in life and he enjoys his food. He was in good spirits. I didn't want to spoil the moment and I wondered if it would rattle his cage to ask him to tell me more about his crimes. I'd heard that he held up a security van in a raid that rivalled the Great Train Robbery. Did he want to talk about it now, though?

'You know most of the Great Train Robbers, don't you, Roy?'

'Yeah,' he replied nonchalantly. 'Been inside with most of them. Ronnie's a good pal of mine. I'm sorry at how it's ended up for him.'

'What was the most you ever got from a robbery?' I asked.

Roy thought for a moment. 'In today's terms, it would be the equivalent of £2 million.'

'A lot of money,' I murmured.

'We'd planned it for a long time. It was an armoured van and we thought our method was foolproof. We weren't going to get caught. Nothing could go wrong. We'd thought of every contingency.'

I knew that Roy had gone to prison for a long time for this robbery. 'So what went wrong?'

Roy leaned forward and grabbed a pen. He started drawing diagrams on the pub menu. 'It was a version of our usual jobs – stop the van with a brick, ram it, then haul the guards out and get the money. See, this is where we were parked and this is where the van came from.'

'But that didn't happen?'

'Sort of. I jumped out and stopped the van all right – I hurled the brick so hard it went straight through the windscreen and hit the driver on the head. That did it. The van careered all over the road, then our ramming van screeched forward but they missed it. I don't know how that happened. What a cock-up – the security van went sailing past us ... it finished up 20 yards away. We all sprinted down there. The driver didn't know where he was or what had happened. He was covered in blood.'

'Did you feel scared?'

Roy looked at me as though I was mad. His face was lit up. 'I felt bloody hyped up. We didn't need any whizz to get us going – the adrenalin did that. I was almost breathless with excitement. The money was there and I was having it.'

'How many were there in the gang?'

'Only four. There were 15 in the Train Robbery.'

'Did they give you the money?'

He shook his head. 'It wasn't as easy as that. I smashed the van up with my club but we couldn't get inside it. I had to run back to fetch my axe.'

'Surely people had seen what had happened. Didn't anyone try to stop you?'

'No way. They'd all scarpered. Anyway, I whacked away at that van until the window gave way and we were in. The guards were cowering. Don't hurt us, take the money, they were pleading with us. It was like a conveyor belt, we chucked the cases full of money from one set of eager outstretched arms to another until it was safely stashed in the van. And then we got the fuck out of there.'

'You got away with it.'

'Almost. There has to be a fucking hero. Some people just can't keep their noses out. There was a bloke following us in a car.

'We stopped the van sharp, it made him skid to a halt, there were black tyre marks on the road. He was an ordinary bloke peering at me through the windscreen. I was there brandishing an axe and running like a madman towards him. You could see the fear in his face.

'What am I doing here? he was thinking and he slammed the car into reverse gear so quick it scrunched the gears. Then he shot back, skidded on to the verge and overturned. If only he'd minded his own business.'

I didn't know what to say. You couldn't make this up.

Roy went on. 'I walked back to the van and got in. It did us a favour because it blocked the road for us. We drove on nice and calm until we came to our decoy vehicle.'

'Which was?'

Roy smiled. 'A coal lorry.'

'That's certainly different,' I told him.

'That's what we thought. Who's going to stop a coal lorry?'

'You got away with it?'

'Covered in coal dust, but with the sweetest haul ever.'

Roy looked thoughtful. 'I bought my first Merc out of my share. For cash. My only worry was which colour to choose.'

'And then ...?'

Roy sighed. 'I was grassed up. The next thing I knew, I was in the dock and the judge was speaking. "This robbery was carried out quite ruthlessly and most of the money is still in the hands of the robbers. I have to deter other people from doing this. Royston Henry Shaw, you will go prison for 15 years. Shaw, you will also serve another three years for grievous bodily harm. The sentences are to run consecutively." Eighteen fucking years. The bastard had sentenced me to 18 years in prison.'

This prison sentence was the start of the most desperate and painful episodes in Roy's life. The memories were all flooding back and Roy was tense, his hands clenched on the table. It was time for emergency measures. I poured him a brandy and he drank it straight off. So I fetched the bottle. I somehow knew that this was going to be a long evening.

CHAPTER 12

FIND THE LADY

IT HAD BEEN NEARLY A MONTH SINCE ROY'S
VISIT AND I WAS DREADING A TELEPHONE CALL.

Roy would ask me about Dorothy and I would have to
admit that I was nowhere in the hunt for her. One of my
researchers had done the initial people search and I'd had
an email from him the previous week. He'd found a
Dorothy Tyler living at 42 Ryebridge Hill. She'd been there
for seven years, living with a guy called Alan Talbot. There
were no Dorothy Talbots so it didn't look as though they
were married.

I'd driven to the address to see if she was still there. It was
suburbia, privet hedges and bay-windowed bungalows.
Somehow, I couldn't imagine Dorothy fitting in here.

She had captured Roy's heart and left a lifelong wound
in it that wouldn't heal. She must be a special lady. I drove

round the estate looking for number 42, clutching a faded photo of a young woman with short brown hair, sparkling eyes and a lovely smile. What if I didn't recognise her? I was almost dreading what I was going to find.

What if Dorothy had drifted into nine-to-five anonymity? Bingo, *Coronation Street*, cutting the lawn and washing the car?

I felt eyes upon me as I parked the car and walked up the street. Twenty-six, thirty-two ... the net curtains were twitching as the occupants peeked at me.

Forty-two. Hmm. It did look a bit different. Not quite hot property but with a certain style. Someone had chopped down the hedge, planted a monkey puzzle tree, painted the front door red. There was a high fence stopping all entrance to the back garden.

And there were no net curtains. The windows had wooden slatted blinds. Closed. It looked odd somehow, a bit offbeat. As though someone had tried to make a difference and then given up.

I took the plunge and walked up the front path and knocked on the door. A dog barked. Yap, yap, yap. I knocked again. Eventually, I could hear footsteps shuffling to the door. Oh no. Dorothy's down on her luck. Unwell perhaps. Not how Roy remembers her.

I held my breath as someone fumbled with the lock and a bolt top and bottom. I could hear soft muttered curses, the door seemed to be sticking. The suspense was killing me; another minute and I was going to give it a push. It opened just a crack, six inches, no more.

And it wasn't Dorothy ... phew! She hadn't changed or aged. It was a bloke, quite a young man actually, looking bleary-eyed, his hair stuck up on end.

'I'm sorry to disturb you,' I told him apologetically. 'I'm looking for Dorothy Tyler ... does she live here?'

He looked back at me as though he didn't understand. Maybe he didn't speak English. I started again, more slowly. 'Her second name might be Talbot. Dorothy Talbot? I was told this was her address.'

The young man must have decided I was safe because he opened the door a bit wider and had a proper look at me. 'I dunno,' he told me at last. 'Dorothy Talbot. No. Never heard of her.'

'Or Tyler ...' I reminded him.

He yawned. 'I work nights. At the hospital.'

Oh sugar. 'I'm sorry. I've woken you up. It's just that it's really important to find Dorothy. My friend's lost track of her. He's desperate to find her. I was told this was her address.'

'No. It isn't now anyway. I only moved here a couple of months ago.'

'You don't know who lived here before?'

He nodded. 'Yeah. A couple of my pals from work shared it. They were here about two years.'

'Is it rented?'

'Yeah.' He yawned again.

'You don't know who owns it, do you?'

He shook his head and rubbed his eyes. I knew I had to let him go back to his kip.

'Thanks, anyway,' I started to say, but the door had already closed.

The next-door neighbour at number 44 was an elderly lady with her hair in curlers. She'd have talked all day and was obviously lonely. She thought she remembered someone called Dorothy living there three or four years ago, a lovely lady, very kind, but time flies, doesn't it, and she wasn't sure. I asked where her nice neighbour had moved on to, just in case.

Derbyshire, she thought, somewhere up north anyway. I had a moment's inspiration. Did the nice lady have a dog? Why, yes, she did. A big dog. It looked a bit fierce but it wasn't really. I asked if it was black-and-tan coloured.

Yes, it sounded like a Rottweiler. Roy's favourite breed. A coincidence? Maybe, but I had a gut feeling I was on the trail. A long way to go, even so.

I drove back home and studied the email again. There was another Dorothy Tyler living in Essex. It didn't seem likely – she was married to a William Tyler. A husband-and-wife team.

We had found out that Dorothy's middle name was Ann so that had narrowed the search. There were three Dorothy Tylers with phone numbers – all living in the South of England. The first one lived in Kent. I decided to ring her.

No reply. I rang again. No reply. By the third day, I had just about decided I'd have to go see for myself. One more try and at last she answered.

'Hello.'

'Is that Dorothy?' I asked in a quiet voice. I'd thought of saying Mrs Talbot or Dorothy Talbot, but if she was wanting to hide, if she was a bit wary, that might put her off. I'd go softly.

'Yes, who's this?' Already she sounded suspicious.

I gave her my name and told her that I was doing some research for my book. Dorothy became quite interested. We talked for a while. Yes, she'd lived in London. Her age was about right. She sounded bright and vivacious. Had she ever had a boyfriend called Roy?

Even that worked out right. Straight off, she told me that she had gone out with Roy, some years earlier. That rang warning bells. She'd answered too easily. Any woman who'd been involved with Roy Shaw would have made more of it. It wouldn't have been a run-of-the-mill experience.

Yet this Dorothy had been unconcerned, unfazed by a relationship with her Roy. I sensed that she wasn't the one I was seeking. She invited me over and I nearly agreed to go. Then the penny dropped. Roy's lost love was born in the South. This Dorothy had a Geordie accent.

I sat down to go through my list again the next evening. Dorothy A Talbot, Salord House, Redhill, Surrey. It was an upmarket address. That figured. Roy had told me Dorothy looked as though she was doing well. There's something about having money that shows – is it the hairdo, the fashionable clothes, the established Caribbean tan, the perfectly manicured nails, discreet 22ct gold jewellery – or is it just the £30,000 motor?

Dorothy could be living high on the hog in leafy Surrey. I picked up the phone.

'Good evening.' I tried to be more formal this time. 'May I speak to Dorothy Talbot please?'

'Si, si, madame. I fetch.'

Hmm. Hired help. I could hear footsteps on a polished floor and then a cultured voice breathed down the phone. 'Hello, sweetie.'

'Is that Dorothy?'

'Camilla?'

'No. Er, it's Kate. Kate Kray.'

I was going to disappoint her. And I did. I don't know which Camilla she was expecting to call, but she certainly wasn't prepared for Kate Kray. Dorothy from Surrey recovered quickly and was nothing if not polite.

'I see.'

I explained about my book and Roy Shaw. 'I'm afraid I've never heard of Mr Shaw,' she told me. 'A boxer, did you say?'

As I recounted my story of lost love, gangsters and the fight game, the 'I sees' became fainter.

In the end, I felt pleased that she'd not heard of either me, Pretty Boy or any other hard bastards and I thanked her profusely and put down the phone. I'd done the sublime ... my next call was ridiculous. Dorothy A Talbot from Marazian in Cornwall.

The number rang a long time before the woman answered. I was ready for a Cornish tinge to the voice but if there was an accent at all it was unfamiliar to me.

My biggest problem was that I'd never met Dorothy. All I had to go on was Roy's glowing description – bright, vivacious, lots to say for herself. I imagined her to be a bit cheeky, able to stand up for herself.

Dorothy from Cornwall fitted the bill perfectly. 'Kate! From off the telly! Wow!'

The problem was that she wanted to talk about me, not her.

'But have you ever lived in London?'

'I was born in London,' she shrieked. And she rabbited on and on. She knew the clubs, the pubs, the hard men. But did she know Roy Shaw?

'When can I see him? Oooh, it's been ages.'

I couldn't weigh up if she was for real. If it had been years since Roy had known her, maybe livewire had turned into tangle. But her age was right, her background was real, she knew lots about the man. I had a sudden inspiration.

'Have you read any books about Roy?' I asked her.

'All of them,' she told me proudly. 'He signed one of them as well. I waited outside Epping Forest Country Club and he talked to me for ages.'

My heart sank. So that was it. I tried one more question, just to make sure. 'Is Talbot your maiden name or your married name?'

'Married. Huh. He was a right bastard. I knew I should have changed it back. But then you wouldn't have found me, would you?'

I sighed. Of all the crazy coincidences. One of Roy's biggest fans had the same married name as his former girlfriend. Dotty Dorothy was still asking me to try to fix her up with a date as I rang off.

Back to the beginning. My researcher had found two Dorothy A Talbots listed in the London area. I got through to both of the numbers without any difficulty at all.

I had to wait for the first one to go and get her hearing aid. 'Hello? Hello? Is that Cathy?'

'No, it's Kate,' I yelled down the handset.

'What time are you coming round? Don't forget my arrowroot biscuits, will you?' Dorothy was very sweet and all of 96 years young. When she'd managed to wire herself for sound, we had a lovely chat.

She thought I was the replacement home help. 'When are you coming to put me to bed?' Her voice was a bit frail.

Miss Dorothy sounded a smashing lady. I felt like going round there and tucking her in straight away. I gave her my phone number and she promised to ring me if the home help didn't turn up.

But I was no nearer to finding the lady.

The last Dorothy A Talbot on my list had a Cockney accent and what sounded like dozens of screaming kids in the background. She told me all in a gabble that there was a six-month-old baby, twin boys aged two-and-a-half, a girl of five and another lad of eight. She was waiting for her mum to come round and give her a hand. We both hoped she'd hurry up.

I put the phone down. I couldn't believe I was drawing such a complete blank. I had another look at the notes. What if ... Dorothy had married Alan Talbot?

Roy would be broken-hearted. Would he still want to find out if it was bad news? Maybe she wasn't alive even. I could pack it in, tell him I couldn't find her. Mmm. But now my curiosity was aroused – what had happened to her? Had she changed her name, was she scarred for life by the Shaw experience – or was there life after Roy?

Anyway, in these computer trail-generating, friends-reuniting, satellite-tracking times, how can anyone disappear like this?

I could try all the right-age Alan Talbots and see if any of those had a wife/partner/girlfriend called Dorothy Ann. There was something niggling me. An elusive clue. Was there another way and I kept missing it? Then it came to me ... I thought about the neighbour who'd known a Dorothy with a Rottweiler dog.

I made myself a cup of coffee while I mulled it over. If you have a dog, you have to be registered with a vet. Mmm. If you change vets – does your dog's record go to the new vet? It seemed logical.

So, if that was the right Dorothy, and if she still had the dog and if she'd changed vets, and if the old vet had passed her records on ... if, if, if ... I might be able to trace her that way. But it was a long shot. What the hell, I decided to go back as soon as I could and talk to that old lady again.

I went to bed thinking about what I was going to tell Roy and wishing I'd never become involved in this. If I didn't suceed, he was going to be so disappointed.

I drifted off to sleep thinking it was pretty hopeless – I might as well have been searching for the Holy Grail.

CHAPTER 13

RONNIE BIGGS –
HE DID THE CRIME
BUT NOT THE TIME

A FEW WEEKS AFTER MY HUNT FOR DOROTHY, I WENT TO SEE ROY AT HIS HOUSE. We'd arranged to meet to talk some more and Roy had invited me for tea.

There was no sign of the dogs when I arrived; they'd been shut into their compound. Roy seemed calm, in a good mood; I hoped it would last.

As he showed me into the sitting room, I kept thinking about what I was going to tell him about my fruitless search for Dorothy but, to my relief, he didn't mention her.

It was all very civilised; it's a beautiful house and we sat in a room with windows overlooking the lawn. Roy brought in a tray of tea and cakes.

I noticed the china; it was lovely, edged with gold and initialled with a crest – RS.

'Personalised cups and saucers?' I asked.

Roy nodded. 'I've a whole dinner service done the same,' he told me. Somehow, I wasn't surprised, although to anyone not knowing him, it would have seemed at odds with his image. On the one hand, here's a man with a harrowing life story and layer upon layer of brutality, hatred and anger. But peel away the layers of violence, madness and sadness and you will find that Roy has endearing qualities. He doesn't blame anyone, it's not his childhood or society. He never avoids the truth because he knows the buck stops with him. Roy is one of the most straightforward and direct men I've ever met. He has never stepped over an invisible mark, or allowed anyone else to. His experiences have made him strong and he's learned from them, good and bad. And he knows how to treat a lady.

'Are you comfy there?' he asked. He made sure the light was OK, not shining in my eyes. Did I want another cushion? Was I warm enough? The perfect host.

Roy is always a gentleman and never uncouth. Whenever we've met, it's been the same, I've found that he is careful not to offend me, because it's not tough or clever to be uncouth.

His looks are at odds with his character and I have always found him to be a contradiction. When Roy bares his soul, it can be a harrowing experience just to listen to him. The emotions are buried deep but, when the protective layers are slowly peeled away, he laughs as well as cries and is embarrassed by neither.

We began to talk about the blokes he'd been in prison

with – and inevitably the man to start with was the infamous Great Train Robber, Ronnie Biggs.

'When did you first meet Ronnie?' I took a sip of my Assam tea and settled back into the sofa.

Roy thought about it for just a moment or two. 'I was in Wandsworth Prison in London. In those days, it was a tough place. It might still be.'

'What was it like?'

'For one thing it was cold. The prisoners weren't allowed to talk and this horrible deathly silence hung over the landings. We were always hungry as well.'

Roy held out a plate of biscuits but I shook my head.

'What was the food like? Was it good?'

He shook his head. 'It was terrible. You never had enough to eat.' He took a sip of his tea. 'There was nothing to eat or drink after you were locked up for the night, sometimes at four-thirty. Except water. You could always have a drink of cold water, though, to keep you going. There was one treat a year and that was on Christmas Day.'

'Turkey and stuffing?'

'Fish and chips,' he said with a shake of his head. 'That was our Christmas dinner.' Roy leaned forward in his chair. 'They had us sewing mailbags. Yeah, it was what you'd expect, I suppose. The policy was to use us as unpaid labour. They gave us menial jobs that people on the outside wouldn't want to do. So one day I was in the mailbag room, sewing away, when who do I find myself sitting next to, but Ronnie Biggs.'

'He was there for the Great Train Robbery?'

'He'd got a 30-year sentence. Right from the word go, Biggsy and I hit it off. We were both Londoners, both robbers and both, unfortunately, in prison.'

'So you had a lot in common?'

'That's right, Katie. And while we were sewing the mailbags every day, he told me about his plan to escape. It was ingenious, it was daring, it was simple.'

'Did you get involved with it?'

'Right from the word go. Ronnie told me he was having it away on his toes and he asked me if I wanted to be in.'

'And did you?'

'I thought about it long and hard. It was going to cost me £10,000.'

'That's what he wanted?'

'There were expenses ... if I wanted in, I had to share them. These things take a lot of arranging. You have to pay people to be where you want them to be. You have to pay people to look the other way. And then there's what happens next. It's not over when you get outside that wall, that's just the start of it. I suppose ten grand wasn't bad in the circumstances.'

'A lot of money at that time.'

'Oh yes. But I had a lot of money,' he said simply. 'What I didn't have was freedom.'

'So you weighed it up?'

He nodded. 'It was 18 years inside or a ten grand ticket to a new life.' Roy paused. 'There's always more to it than that, of course.'

'If you get caught?'

'Your sentence is going to be longer. But not only that, it's your family. Your friends. They can't go with you. They're the link, it's how they trace you. So I had a long hard think. I knew that ten grand would just get me over the wall. Then I'd need a forged passport, money for tickets to go abroad, a new identity.'

'Would this have been easy to do?'

'It's not impossible, but it costs money. When people know your circumstances, the prices go sky high. It's human nature.'

'So there was a lot against it.'

'Yeah. But when you're inside and facing a long sentence, when a thought like this gets into your head, you can't get it out. It was all Biggsy and I talked about. He'd got it sussed. He told me all about it, the inside and out of a duck's arse and more. He was going to travel to Holland in a cargo ship, then he was going to Paris and having plastic surgery.'

'To change his appearance?'

'Nothing too radical I don't think. A face-lift. Then he was going to disappear in Australia for a while.'

'It's a big country,' I murmured. 'I suppose anyone could lose themselves there.'

'With the right papers, no doubt about it,' Roy went on. 'Ronnie had left nothing to chance. It was all planned meticulously.'

'Did he intend to stay in Aussie Land?'

'No, that was never on the cards. It was a stopping-off

place. He'd always meant to go to South America. He was going to Panama, Caracas and finally Rio de Janeiro. I think he knew that was where he'd really be safe. The one place they couldn't get him. It was where your pound note went a long way.'

I wondered how would Roy have coped with it. 'Rio's a long way from London. Would you have liked all the travelling about?'

Roy stood up and walked to the window. 'I wouldn't have minded, if I could have got my family out there with me eventually.'

'So, you'd made your mind up to go?'

Roy turned back to face me. 'Yeah. I didn't want to think about 18 years being taken out of my life. I was up for it. I told him I was in.'

'What happened?'

Roy shrugged. 'The best laid plans and all that. The powers that be suddenly decided they didn't want me in Wandsworth any more. They moved me to Her Majesty's big house on the Isle of Wight. The decision was taken away from me. That's how it happens. In prison, you're nobody. They can do anything they like with you, send you anywhere or leave you to fester in a rat hole. You don't exist any more.'

'But Ronnie did get away?'

'Oh yeah. I was lying on my bunk one day when another prisoner came in and said, "Ronnie Biggs has gone over the wall."'

'I bet that made you smile.'

'It did as well. I bet he felt like Steve McQueen in *The Great Escape*. After that, I spent many nights through my prison sentence thinking about it.'

'Wishing you'd gone with him?'

'Yes. I envied him. I wished I'd taken him up on his offer straight away. I'd have been out of there before they could have moved me on.'

'You had a lot of time to think?'

'You've nothing to occupy your mind in prison. You don't have to take responsibility for anything. Not where your next meal is coming from. You don't have anywhere to go, nothing to do, you haven't got a bus or a train to catch. When you're alone in your cell at night and the doors are banged shut and you know there's no way you can get out of there, the only way to stop yourself going insane is to let your mind wander. I used to go somewhere different every night. White beaches and blue sea ... suntanned young women sitting beside me under a palm tree ... sipping a margarita. If only.'

'I bet you never thought that you'd really be doing that a few years into the future?'

'I hoped. I've always had a lot of confidence in myself. But you never know what's around the corner.'

'It was one dream that came true for you.'

Roy has been on some fabulous holidays in the sun. 'I was pleased for Biggsy,' he went on. 'Managing to elude the Metropolitan Police for so long. I have to take my hat off to the man.'

'Thirty-four years, wasn't it?'

'Something like that. Although he's back inside now, which is sad. They seem determined to punish him for ever.'

There was a phone ringing in another room and Roy excused himself to go and answer it. He came back in.

'A boxing match I've been invited to in Birmingham. Are you all right for a few minutes?'

I asked Roy if he would sort it for me to speak to Ronnie Biggs. Within a matter of moments, Ronnie was on the phone telling me all about Roy.

We kept in touch and had a chat on the phone several times after that. Ronnie was always ready to talk; I think he missed the old days and friends from the past. He'd told me all about his time in Wandsworth and how he planned his escape.

'I hated Wandsworth, and so did Roy. We were on the A-list together.'

'The A-list? Is that for blokes who're really good?'

Ronnie had laughed. He is a light-hearted individual and always cheerful. 'Not quite, Kate. It's for prisoners who are put on a special watch because they've escaped or tried to escape or they think they might escape.'

'They were keeping their eye on you.'

'Yes. It didn't do them any good though, did it?'

'Were you trying to get away right from the start?'

'I'd had offers to escape from the first day almost, but most of them weren't worth listening to, except one I received. I liked the sound of it because it was simple. I didn't think anything could go wrong. And it didn't.'

'Did you always intend to go on your own?'

'No,' Ronnie told me. 'I was on good terms with Roy. I'd heard about his reputation before I met him. We got on well and I thought that he would be very handy if we had any problems.'

'When you were escaping?'

'Yes, with the screws. If there was any trouble, Roy would be able to take care of it. I knew I'd be able to depend on him.'

'When you say that, what exactly do you mean?'

Ronnie hesitated. 'You know what he's like, Kate. If anyone had tried to stop us, he wouldn't have taken the time to argue it out with them. But that was the whole point, nobody would have tried to stop Roy.'

'He was unstoppable?'

'Yes, he didn't mess about and everyone knew that. The screws, the lot of them.'

'What would he have done?'

Ronnie wasn't to be drawn. 'I don't want to go into that. I would have felt better if he'd been along. Any trouble anywhere and he'd have taken care of it.'

'But he was transferred before you were ready.'

'Yes, that's the way it is. I had to go it alone. The rest is history.'

'It worked out all right for you.'

'I got away, didn't I?'

Was there just the tiniest hint of regret in his voice? It's hard to tell when you're not face to face. Ronnie Biggs has always shown a brave face to the world.

'It must have been disappointing for Roy. He had to serve his sentence.'

'Yes, he had it rough. I heard about it.'

So the prison grapevine stretches right round the world.

'But we've had some good times since,' Ronnie went on. 'Roy came out to see me in Rio.'

'What did you think? Had he changed?'

Ronnie told me that Roy was exactly the same, as big as ever, if not bigger. 'Characters like Roy never alter. He seemed larger than life. Especially in Rio. We picked up where we left off.'

'You'd have a lot to talk about. Did Roy stay with you?'

'No, he had a reservation at the Sheraton. I had some guests staying with me, Nick Reynolds the sculptor and his friend who was a photographer. He was called Anthony. They wanted to do a photo shoot of Roy.'

Ronnie told me they'd all had Christmas dinner together – a fabulous time, he said; it sounded as though they'd all enjoyed it.

'Did you go out on the town?' I asked. Roy likes to party and I didn't believe that Ronnie was averse to a little bit of nightlife. But he wouldn't be drawn.

'You'd better ask him about it, Kate,' he told me.

I took that as a 'yes'.

'Was that the only time Roy went out to see you?'

'No, he came over again – for my birthday. Now that was a bit of a "do". Roy entertained us by showing us his party tricks, eating champagne glasses among other things! It turned into a birthday I'll never forget.'

I sensed a wistful tone in his voice. Maybe a sense of what might have been crept over him when he talked about old times. People might envy him his life in the sun, but I thought it had been a sentence in a way, cut off from everybody he knew. In any event, he'd had enough reminiscing. He began to edge out of the call and make his excuses, places to go, people to see. Ronnie Biggs wished me well, sent his regards to Roy and put the phone down. Was it really business deals and important appointments or would he be drifting back to the bar stool in a downtown club and trying not to think about the past?

Roy came back in looking pleased with himself.

'You look like a man who's done a good deal.'

'I like to earn a quid or two,' he told me with a sparkle in his eye.

'There's nothing like a straight pound note,' I said.

'We'll drink to that,' he agreed, walking over to the sideboard and getting out two tall champagne glasses. I was about to say, 'No, not for me, I'm driving,' when I realised that he was pouring organic grape juice. Roy is a health food fanatic. He exercises, does weights and watches his diet. Keeping that famous body in good shape is high priority. But what about Rio? What did Roy remember about his South American trip?

'It was good to see Biggsy again. In a way, he hadn't changed. He seemed to be enjoying life. But it's different over there.'

'Were you glad in retrospect that you hadn't escaped with him?'

Roy didn't hesitate. 'Yes. Although it would have saved me a lot of grief. It's isolated from everyone you know. It was a good holiday, though.'

'What did you do?'

'Ronnie showed me the Copacabana nightlife. The weather wasn't so good and it started to piss it down with rain so we had to take shelter. All the hookers go into the bars on the seafront when it rains and we went to one of them.'

'A wild night in Rio,' I murmured.

'Something to remember.' Roy nodded. 'I went back to see him on his birthday. Did he tell you?'

I liked the casual way Roy talked about flying halfway round the world.

'Yes, he said you would tell me all about the party ...'

I looked at him expectantly but he coloured slightly.

'Some other time, Katie,' he told me, looking at his gold Piaget. 'Look, it's turned six. Do you fancy going out for something to eat? We can talk some more over a meal.'

It was an offer I couldn't refuse.

CHAPTER 14

THE BAD, THE BAD
AND THE UGLY

ROY TOOK ME TO THE ROCHESTER GRILL, AN UPMARKET RESTAURANT IN THE CENTRE OF TOWN. They knew who he was. 'Welcome, Mr Shaw. Come in. How are you?' We were ushered to a table in the far corner. There was a crisp, white linen tablecloth, silver cutlery and a good view of the door. Was this just a coincidence or do old habits die hard?

We ordered, lemon sole for me and Steak Diane for Roy. The food was as plentiful and good as the old oak panelling, deep-pile carpet and discreet, attentive service suggested.

We ate almost in silence – pass the salt ... more mineral water ... would you like a pudding?

I managed to resist both the Chocolate to Die For and the Tiramisu but threw in the towel at the Irish coffee round. Roy went the distance, ordering apple crumble with custard, a straight coffee and a brandy to round it off. Eventually, he settled back in his chair and smoothly took up where he'd left off earlier. We whizzed back in time to Borstal and he began telling me all about how he became a prison daddy before he became a real daddy.

'I was on my first day in Borstal. It was at a barrack of a dump in Wales, at a place called Usk. There was the prison – they called it the Jug, and then they had the camp.

'The night I arrived, there was a boxing competition between the camp and the Jug. Some of the boys from the camp came up to me and they said, "You've done a bit of boxing, haven't you, Shaw?" It was no use denying it. I wasn't going to anyway. Boxing was life's blood to me.'

'You were up for it?'

'I was. Well, they wheeled out their best man. He was the daddy of the camp.'

'What does that mean – "daddy"?'

'The bloke in charge – the one who runs it.'

'Don't the prison officers run it?'

'They like to think they do. But the truth is, they don't. When you're inside, there's hundreds of us and only a few of them.'

'That's true.' I'd never thought about it like that before.

'There has to be someone to keep the boys in line. Sort out arguments.'

'And that's the daddy?'

'That's what he's called. Anyway, they fetched this guy up and we had a bit of a spar. I gave him a little tap – Bang! Bang! – and over he goes. I couldn't believe it. But that wasn't it. Then the daddy of the Jug comes up. He says to me, "Oy, you've taken liberties there, you'll have to have it out with me now." '

'Was that as easy?'

'I looked him up and down. This was the real thing. I knew I'd have a fight on my hands, so I just went out and bashed him and it was over. I'd done it. I'd beat their best and there I was, the first day and I was the daddy of the whole place.'

'Impressive.'

Roy downed his drink and shrugged. 'They couldn't really fight. Big fish in little ponds.'

'What did it mean to you? Did you get lots of privileges?'

'I never took advantage of it,' Roy told me. 'Lots of daddies make the guys clean their room and run about after them, make their tea, that sort of thing. I never did anything like that. I got respect and that was enough.'

'What about prison? Did you have to fight in there as well?'

Roy's expression hardened. 'That's different. No choice. You have to. It's dog eat dog in the nick. If you don't get yourself established, it's all over. You know, you get the little gangs. Some of them think they're tougher than all the others. They want to prove it. In the early stages, you have to fight to show them what you're made of – when it gets around that you've done a few, they leave off. You get, "Shaw can have a row, leave him alone." '

'Your reputation goes before you?'

'That's it.'

I thought about this for a while. Roy ordered more coffee. It struck me that since the early days, he has always been a loner. 'Were you ever in a gang in prison?' I asked him.

He shook his head. 'I like to think I can rely on myself.'

'Is that how you prefer to be ... it's all down to you?'

Roy sighed. 'Always. I don't need a gang. Whatever I've done, I've done myself.'

That was so true. There was no stopping Roy now.

'I've bought properties. Not on the never never. I've paid for them with money I've earned. And I've done them up myself and sold them.'

'You're a property entrepreneur.'

'That's the fancy way to put it.'

'But fighting's been the most important thing to you?'

'Without a doubt. I had ten pro fights when I was with Mickey Duff.'

'He was your trainer?'

'Yes. Ten wins and six knockouts.'

'Were you fighting under your own name?'

Roy shook his head. 'No, I was under the name Roy West.' He gave a quick smile. 'I was on the run. People were looking for Roy Shaw.'

'What weight did you fight at then?'

'I was a middleweight. That was my natural weight.'

'What about the fighting outside the ring?'

'In the street? I was always having punch-ups.'

I looked down at his massive fists; touch them and they are as hard as iron. 'Are you a right-hander?'

'Yeah. It's a lot different in the street from in the ring. In a boxing match, you're moving around a lot, getting set for a punch. But in the street you're usually stationary. It's like doing it from nothing. The power comes from your legs and your body. You have to put everything into it – full blast.'

'Has that always worked for you?'

Roy nodded. 'Always. Without a doubt.'

There have been a lot of famous punch-ups in Roy's career. I decided to ask him about them. 'Is it true, Roy, that you once took on four blokes at one time?'

His face widened into a smile.

'How can anyone fight four people together?'

'I'll tell you how it happened. We were in a restaurant. I was with my wife, it was before we split up. My mate was there with his wife. A nice ordinary outing.'

'Until ...'

'Until,' Roy said, 'this geezer pushed my mate's missus and he says, "Hoy, hoy, turn it up." '

'He meant watch what you're doing?'

'That's right. We just went on, having a chat, having a drink. We were about to leave as a matter of fact. The girls fancied a bit of dancing. We were going to a nightclub. But one of these blokes is coming the big man. "What's the matter with you, son?" he says. I gave him a look, but we'd got the women with us and we didn't want any trouble. It was a night out and we were enjoying ourselves. We started to walk away.'

'They wouldn't let it go?'

Roy with Dorothy – but where is she now?

Top: Joe Pyle announces the champion, with Dorothy by Roy's side.

Bottom: The advert Roy placed for Dorothy.

DOROTHY
Will you marry me.
Get some
happiness into
your life.
Roy. xxxxx

Top: Roy with the bubbly Barbara Windsor.

Bottom: Roy with another EastEnder – Daniella Westbrook.

Fun in the sun with Brazil's most famous import – Ronnie Biggs.

The note on this photo from Ronnie Biggs reads: 'To me old mate Roy (something to throw darts at!) Ronnie Biggs.'

Top: Soaking up the sun. (*Left to right*) Ronnie Biggs, Roy, Anthony Oliver and Nicky Reynolds.

Bottom: Re-living the old times with, among others, Tony Lambrianou and Freddie Foreman.

Right: Roy is still a legendary name on the boxing circuit – this is the programme for a boxing event hosted by him.

Top: Roy with his old school pals at a school reunion.

Bottom: Roy with Joe Pyle and Gillian Taylforth.

Roy's million-pound house.

'Not a chance. They wanted a row. The four of them came after us. We told the girls to get in the car and they scarpered sharp-ish. I whispered to my mate, "I'll take the biggest," and I turned round with my fists up. I didn't wait, I leaped across the pavement and took the fight to him. Whack! I slammed into him with my right hand, and this big one, he was down. The others were squaring up to me and I went over to the next one, hit him with a left hook and he was down. My mate was having a scuffle and I went to give him a hand.

'I put him on the floor and that left one. He was a bit uncertain by now but I made his mind up for him. I landed him a punch right on his jaw – he went out like a light. That was the four of them.'

All the time he was telling me this, Roy had been clenching and unclenching his fists, his eyes on fire; in his head, he was still fighting them. But he never told me in a bragging sort of way. Just relived it so I could get the story right.

'Where does this punch come from, Roy?' Everyone talks about his massive knockout blows. 'Is it something you were born with – or did you learn how to do it?'

'You can develop it, but I think it is a gift. You either have it or you don't. It's nothing to do with size. Maybe it's attitude. Jimmy Wilde was only a lightweight but he could knock out middleweights and even heavyweights.'

'Was that because he had the gift?'

'Undoubtedly. Have you heard of Joe Erskine?'

My partner Leo was a boxer so I know most names involved in the fight game. 'Yes, the Welsh heavyweight.'

Roy nodded. 'He was a fantastic boxer but there was one flaw. He couldn't punch. He was a very clever tactical fighter. If he could have punched, he'd have been world class. Then you had Henry Cooper with his left hook. There was no doubt about that – Bang! and it was there. It is a gift.'

'I know that you'd been barred from going professional but how did you actually get into the bare-knuckle fighting? It's something most people don't hear about.'

Roy rubbed his chin. Maybe this was something he hadn't thought about for a while. 'I'd bought some property and I was doing something I hadn't done for a long while.'

'What was that?'

Roy smiled. 'Carrying bricks. I was doing the donkey work myself. I was building an extension on the house. I didn't mind, I was enjoying myself. Working for somebody else is a pain in the arse. But when it's for yourself ...'

'That's different.' I agreed. 'You like doing property up?'

'I do. You improve something. It's your own labour, your own plan. It's sound and it's refurbished. Then you sell it and have a big draw. Not bad.'

Well, that's one way to describe the property business. Oversimplifying perhaps. But Roy has a way of getting down to basics in whatever he does.

Roy went on, 'I was doing a bit of pointing and a mate came round to see me. He told me there were going to be some fights arranged at Barnet Fair. He asked me why I didn't have a go. "You could earn yourself a few quid," he told me. I thought about this. I needed money for the house, so I decided to have a go.'

'What sort of fights were they?'

'Very loose. A geezer would say, "My son can beat your son," or "My guy can beat you," and they'd say, "All right," and they'd have a wager on it.'

'Did you bet on yourself?'

Roy smiled. 'I won six grand in the afternoon. Three fights. That's all it took.'

'That made your reputation.'

'Not half.'

'Was it easy money? What I mean to say is, were they easy fights?'

Roy looked thoughtful. 'Those first three were exceptionally easy. I had the advantage. I was a pro fighter. The fights only lasted three or four punches. But other fights, later, were more difficult. I don't know whether any fight should really be called easy. A fight's a fight. It's you or the other guy. Some of them could have a scrap but I still had the advantage. I knew how to pace myself, how to punch and pick my punches. I had a terrific advantage.'

'You fought Donny Adams?'

'The King of the Gypsies, they called him.'

'Had you met up with him before?'

'Yes. I'd been in prison with him. He was a big powerful fella. He was on punishment most of the time.'

'Why was that?'

'He kept hitting the screws.'

'Just like ...' Roy's face was set in a harsh expression ... I let the words trail away.

'Then I fought Lenny McLean. That made me the Guv'nor.'

'Who was it after that?'

Roy grinned. 'Mad Dog Mullins.'

'Mm. Mad Dog. Sounds intimidating.'

'An Irish Guy with a big following. There were people there who backed him for 20 grand.'

'They must have felt confident.'

'Yeah. When I saw him, I did as well. We had a meet in a pub in Notting Hill. Someone said, "Here he comes," and then this little Paddy walked in! And I said "Where's Mullins then?" '

I had to smile. 'I bet that went down well.'

'It set the scene, Katie.' Roy took a last sip of his brandy. 'He was dead serious, though. He said, "I'm Paddy Mullins." He hadn't taken any offence. I couldn't believe it. He was skipping about and sweat was pouring off his face. And that was before the fight.'

'You beat him.'

'I did. Then I fought Terry Hollingsworth. A real tall geezer. I had to work to the body, I smashed him and he crumpled. Then I went for his chin and he went down and it was over.'

'So he lost his money as well?'

'Yes, and I was earning all the time.'

'There wasn't anyone you couldn't fight?'

'No. Tall, short, wiry, stocky. No problem. Towards the

end of my career, I fought a geezer called Lou Yates. He was a thick-set fella, almost as broad as he was tall. He looked the part. But I done him in three rounds.'

'How did you keep so fit when you were in prison?'

'I trained on the weights and power lifting. I could bench-press 365lb, squat 500 and dead-lift 600.'

'They're good poundages.'

'That was on prison food, too.'

'What sort of routine did you follow?'

'Low reps, heavy weights. I only did the dead-lift once a week. But I was training nearly every day, bench-press and squats nearly all the time. I used to do sets of three, then put more weight on and try to squeeze two out and then, before I finished, I'd knock a bit of weight off and do a set of 20.'

It sounded too much like hard work. 'Did you enjoy it?'

'Oh yeah. Yeah. And it helped me get rid of all the aggression.'

I knew that Roy had worked the doors when he was out of prison. I wanted him to tell me about it. 'Did you have many fights when you were on the doors?'

'No, only about three or four. I think it was my reputation. There'd be a bit of aggro building up and I'd go over there and say, "Oy, boys, now turn it in."'

'And they did?'

'Oh yes. If there was going to be ruck, you could almost smell it out, you know, the atmosphere and everything. And I'd go over and say, "All right, boys, turn it in," and they'd say, "All right, Roy, all right." Good as gold.'

'But the fights you did have, what happened there? Was it people pushing their luck?'

Roy loosened his shirt collar. 'Yeah, I suppose. One of the fights was at a club called Jody's. I was minding the place and I was down there, it was pretty crowded. I had a look round and I couldn't believe it, there was Lenny McLean's brother. He was a big flash bloke in those days, a bruiser – a real ugly character. But what was I to do? He was spoiling for causing trouble. I went across to him. I knew I'd have to square him up. I said to him, "Behave yourself or you're going out." He was a bit full of himself. He said to me, "Who's going to put me out?" '

'Brave or foolish,' I murmured.

'Foolish,' Roy said emphatically. 'Anyway,' he went on. 'By now, everybody's turned round to look at us. He was mouthing off, telling me what he was going to do to me.'

'What did you do?'

'I hit him hard. Bang! Down he went. Then I took hold of his leg and dragged him out.'

It sounded like a fight scene from a Spanish Western – the bad, the bad and the ugly.

Roy carried on with his story. 'I had no hassles after that. Everyone in the club had seen me do the big fella and they didn't want any of it. And that's how it was with me in the clubs, you know ... respect.

'One time I was in a club called The Cricketers. They had a little team come in, game boys they thought they were, and they'd had a bit too much and one of them started taking his trousers down. So the bouncer couldn't have that and he went over and started whacking him. And they said, "Right, we'll be back, we're gonna shoot you."'

'Empty threats?' I asked.

'You hear it every day.' Roy shook his head gravely. 'But this was the one time that was different. They went and got their guns and came back. They knocked on the door and the doorman opened it and they shot him dead. They got done for murder.'

I gulped.

'I looked after the club after that.'

'What would you have done in that sort of situation?'

'I would have handled it differently, that's for sure. It's just *how* you handle it. How you handle the situation.' Roy started to get up from the table. 'Will you excuse me for a minute, Katie?' he said. Some people had just come in and a bloke was beckoning him across. 'I've got a bit of business to see to.'

I didn't mind. The place was filling up; we'd dined early and I was ready to start the journey home. So far, Roy hadn't mentioned Dorothy and that was how I meant to keep it. I drank the last of my coffee and was about to get up myself when I felt a hand on my shoulder.

'Kate, you're not going, are you? I wanted to have a word with you.' The voice was gritty, determined. I looked round apprehensively.

It was Terry Spinks.

CHAPTER 15

BOUNCING BACK

I WAS ALL SMILES WHEN I TURNED AND SAW TERRY SPINKS. He was born in 1938 and, having turned to professional boxing, became the ABA Flyweight Champion, the British Featherweight Champion, and an Olympic Gold Medal winner.

'Hello, Terry, how are you?' We gave each other a peck on the cheek.

'I didn't expect to see you here, Kate,' he told me, smiling away.

'I'm here with Roy,' I said, pointing to the bar. He was standing with a group of men who couldn't be anything other than retired boxers, bullet-heads, wide shoulders and systematically rearranged faces. They were jabbing and punching the air and telling the tale; I didn't have to guess that it was the fight game they were talking about. What else would it be when these guys get together?

Terry nodded. 'I had a word with Roy on my way in. And then I spotted you sitting over here all on your own.'

Terry has always been a bit of a charmer, the smiling image of cheeky innocence. He sat down opposite me at the table.

'What are you doing here?' I asked. 'A long way from home, aren't you?' Terry is a Cockney through and through. He was born in the East End of London, the son of a street bookie from Canning Town, he ran bets in the playground from the age of eight, was a jockey at Newmarket in his teens and was working as a binman when the call came to say he'd been selected for the Olympics.

Although Terry took a different path in life, his background is much like Roy's. At various stages, life kicked both these men in the teeth, but they are fighters and were not going to give in.

Down but never out, they struggled and fought their way back, overcoming obstacles that would have killed lesser men, and eventually made it to the top of the heap again. Inevitably, there is a price to pay. And if Roy's is the inability to show emotion, Terry's is more physical.

He ended up as a long-term patient in a clinic for brain injuries. With the help of his cousin, Rosemary, he made a miraculous recovery. Like Roy, he is a tireless fundraiser, raising thousands of pounds for children's charities. And unfortunately, it was one of these charity nights that caused him to get on the wrong side of the authorities. You can't beat the system. These fight game blokes always think they can. Roy was a naughty lad and couldn't get a licence to box professionally. Terry made the mistake of being photographed with the Kray twins. Although he'd won a gold medal in the Olympic Games for his country, it was 45 years before he finally got his due. Was he passed over year after year because of his humble origins – or was it that photo?

After endless campaigning by his friends and supporters, Terry was finally awarded the MBE for his services to sport and charity in the New Year's Honours List in 2001. So I was talking to Terry Spinks MBE. At last.

'Is this one of your old haunts then, Terry?' I asked him.

He nodded. 'Yes, I often come up for a meal with a few old pals,' he said. 'But I think Roy's collared them tonight.'

I'd heard that Terry had been unwell and I was surprised how good he looked. The old sparkle was still in the eyes behind the spectacles although he was a bit heavier than when I'd seen him last.

'I'm 11 stone now,' he patted his midriff. 'I'm making a comeback,' he kidded, 'a middleweight this time.' He's always been known for his sense of humour. He looked at the table and noticed that I didn't have a glass. 'Can I get you a drink, Kate?'

I shook my head. 'Thanks, but I'd better not. We've finished our meal. I have a long drive home.' Terry was holding a glass of what looked like lager. His life, like Roy's, has been a terrifying roller-coaster ride of highs and lows. I'd heard about his long relationship with scotch and that he'd lost most of his middle age. They say that boxing is a sport that makes and breaks and Terry came very close to the edge.

'We never had the chance to have a talk at your book launch,' I told him.

'I was sorry about that. I couldn't get through the crowds.' He'd been surrounded by folk wishing him well and asking him to sign copies of his biography.

'Don't worry about it. There were a lot of people turned up.'

Few people in the boxing world have engendered as much lasting camaraderie as Terry Spinks.

'It was good to see so many old friends,' he told me with a smile.

'I thought there was going to be a fight over the food. It was a stampede when they took that Bacofoil off.'

Terry laughed. He still looks enviably fresh-faced with a full head of hair and barely a wrinkle. Only his realigned nose gives his trade away.

'Did Roy enjoy it?' he asked.

'Oh yes. Any opportunity to talk about boxing. And I managed to chat to quite a few of the guys. They told me a lot I didn't know about Roy. A man of hidden depths.'

'And a few.' Terry laughed. 'What a bloke. A real man's man.'

'You've known Roy a long time. Do you remember much about the early days? When he was boxing?'

Terry leaned back in his chair. 'I remember the old days ... it's yesterday I have trouble with.'

The days when he was living hard had taken its toll on him. At one stage in his life, he lost everything – business, money and family. Roy had turned to crime, Terry had gone down other paths. But both of them had bounced back.

'It was such a pity that he couldn't get his licence. I saw him fight and I never saw a tougher man. He had a rare punch and was as hard as nails.'

'Do you think he'd have made World Champion?' I asked.

Terry nodded. 'If he could have got his licence. That was the problem. It was a catch 22 situation. His fights were legendary. He did bare-knuckle and unlicensed matches. If he'd had his licence it would have been a different story.'

'Do you think he would have stayed away from crime?'

Terry shrugged. 'Who knows? He'd have had no need to do it, would he? Roy could have earned anything he wanted as a professional boxer.'

'Did you ever talk to people who knew him in prison?'

'We all knew the stories about Roy. It used to spread on the grapevine through the East End and the fight world in general. I heard once he put a pool table on his back and broke down a prison wall in a riot.'

That was something I didn't know. Had he caused the riot? With Roy, anything is possible.

'Nothing fazed him. He trod his own path.' Terry gave one of his cheeky grins. 'He might have trod on one or two as well, on the way.'

No doubt about it. 'Anyone who gets in his way,' I agreed. 'Were you a bit of a rascal, in your day then, Terry?'

'Not compared to blokes like Roy. He did armed robberies, blags. No, that wasn't my style. I've never done anything illegal, I've never had so much as a parking ticket.'

'You're known as a bit of a playboy, aren't you?'

'Former playboy,' he told me with a twinkle in his eye. 'I used to gamble. I lost thousands. Everything I'd made. I worked as a bookmaker. A disaster. Then I bought a pub.'

'How did that work out?' What a choice of business venture for a man who's noted for his generosity and for imbibing prodigious quantities of black and tans.

He took a swig of his non-alcoholic lager. 'Another disaster. I drank the profits,' he told me, smiling ruefully.

Is it something about men who have larger-than-life personalities? They make it to the top, but when they crash, it is catastrophic.

Roy would be the first to admit that he was his own worst enemy. He couldn't help himself, couldn't stop getting into nightmare situations, couldn't control his anger. Terry was on a similar downhill spiral. But they both have that special something in them that won't be beaten. Do all boxers have this, or only the great ones? Whatever it is, they've had the courage to claw their way back to the top.

Terry seemed quite content to go on chatting for the rest of the night, but out of the corner of my eye, I saw that

Roy was starting to break away from the group. He'd be heading in our direction in a minute or two.

'I have to start back soon, Terry. It's been great talking to you.' I wished him every success with all his ventures. 'One last thing,' I asked. 'Do you know any secrets about Roy?'

Terry thought about this, he looked puzzled. 'Secrets? No, I don't know him well enough for that.'

'I don't mean anything serious. It might be something that isn't generally known?'

'Ah.' Terry adjusted his spectacles and leaned forward. 'Did you hear about what happened on that bank job?'

I shook my head. 'Tell me, quick, he's coming back.'

Terry lowered his voice. 'One of the geezers doing it with him got wounded and Roy picked him up with one hand and shot back with the other.'

'It's like something out of a *Dirty Harry* movie.'

Terry nodded. 'He's been out there and done it all. Shoot-outs, the lot. But he's a true gentleman. Very well dressed. And when it's party time, he'll sing karaoke with the rest of them.'

'Would you say he's a ladies' man?'

Terry looked past me. 'Roy, how are you, old son?'

The two men shook hands. 'I was just talking to Kate about you,' Terry said.

'My ears are burning,' Roy growled. 'What are you telling her, you old rascal?'

'Only good things, mate. That you're a bit of a ladies' man,' Terry told him. 'And a one hundred per center.'

'That'll do.' Roy sat down, beaming.

They were soon chatting away – re-hashing deals, money, past mayhem. I seized my chance and stood up.

Roy turned to me. 'Kate, just a minute ... I wanted to ask ...'

I looked at my watch. 'Oh no, look at the time. I'm late. Thanks for the meal and everything, Roy. It was great.'

'What about ...?' he persisted.

'I'll ring you,' I interrupted him as I grabbed my coat from the back of the chair. 'There you are, I'm off now.' I said my goodbyes and practically ran to the door.

'Kate ...' I heard Roy calling. 'Have you ...?'

I didn't pause or look back. I wanted to be out of there as quickly as possible. I knew what Roy wanted to ask me. There was only one thing on his mind. Had I found Dorothy for him? But I'd drawn a complete blank. Dorothy had disappeared so successfully that I'd begun to doubt that she had ever existed. I didn't know how Roy was going to take this news but, although I wasn't terribly optimistic, there were one or two more leads to follow up. I felt like disappearing myself, after all my confidence at the outset. I just wasn't ready to tell Roy that this was one find the lady who didn't want to be found.

CHAPTER 16

RUNNING RIOT

ROY CAME DOWN TO THE PUB TO SEE ME A COUPLE OF WEEKS LATER. As soon as he walked through the door, he asked me the question I'd been dreading.

'Have you found her?'

I started to explain but Roy was having none of it. He didn't want to talk about it, he had no interest in the difficulties I faced finding this unfindable lady; there was only one thing he wanted to know – did I know where she was? If I didn't, then he didn't want explanations.

As soon as he learned that I was no nearer to her address or her phone number or where she was, he switched off. That was the end of it. For the time being at least. The dogs ran up to him like a long-lost friend and he helped himself to a ham sandwich from the kitchen and shared it between them. I began to realise that he compartmentalises his life. Roy makes the most of the present and what he can't change he accepts. It's an enviable philosophy. Roy was in an unusually-easy-going mood and it was a lovely blue-sky, sunshiny day. He nodded amiably and agreed to everything I suggested.

Coffee? OK. Anything to eat? Whatever's going. Shall we sit outside? All right.

Maybe he was feeling down because he couldn't have what he really wanted. I began to feel a twinge of guilt for raising his hopes about finding his elusive former girlfriend. Had I underestimated the importance of what this meant to him? This man had health, strength, respect and the confidence that came with surviving the twists and turns of fortune. He had or could get everything else that life could offer – money, travel, big cars, designer clothes, a luxurious home and ... no one to share it with. Was that the problem – even if he didn't want to admit it to himself?

Roy will never give in to the slightest weakness. He never has. But now the thing he wanted was out of reach and I could see that it was gnawing away at him. I didn't want to bring the subject up again. I resolved that I was going to get back on the case as soon as I could. How could she have disappeared? What if she was ...? No. I pushed the thought out of my mind.

We drank our coffees in silence for a few minutes. Then I decided to ask him about his old mates, the past, anything he liked to get his mind away from his problems.

'You were in a lot of prisons, Roy. You must have met most of the notorious gangsters in those days.'

He nodded. 'Yeah. There were some crazy characters.'

'Which was the worst prison?'

Roy gave me a hard look. 'They're all as bad. Once you're inside and they lock that door ...' His voice trailed off. There was more silence, then he started telling me about Maidstone. 'It's in the middle of the town. Literally. It's like a solid fortress, made of stone. It's not only the prison, all the buildings are the same, a particular type of sandstone. It's noisy ... well, all prisons are noisy, but Maidstone is surrounded by traffic – there's a one-way system in the town and the prison is a sort of traffic island right in the middle of it. No matter where you want to go, you have to go round the prison.'

'People driving past forget that there's a prison?'

'Yeah, they're whizzing up and down ... I suppose they're oblivious to the secret life going on right under their noses.'

'Can you see outside?'

'Some of the cells have windows overlooking the main road.'

'You can see life going on around you?' I couldn't decide whether this was good or bad.

Roy nodded. 'It makes it more difficult in a way. If you're serving a long sentence, you're witnessing the normal world. For a lifer especially. He can see everything he wants and can't have. He knows he might never get it back. Normal life.'

'We take it for granted on the outside.'

'In prison, you remember certain things – they stick in your mind long after you've done your sentence. In Maidstone, it's market day on Tuesday and the whole town is a hustle and bustle. It seems to penetrate the cells and filter into the mind of every con.

'There's a smell of food cooking, roast potato stalls and hamburger stands – this is torture for all the cons whose only thought is their next meal. You're always hungry in prison. The prisons are run on a tight budget. I think food must be at the bottom of the list. They allocate a minute amount to feed the blokes. It's never enough.'

'Was Maidstone the first prison you went to after Borstal?'

'It was. I was a young offender entering a man's world, but I was ready. I knew I could deal with whatever lay ahead of me.'

'Was it a tough prison?'

Roy gave a bitter laugh. 'If I was looking for trouble, I'd come to the right place. It was full of hard-nosed cons who thought they could chew anyone up and spit them out.'

'Did they try with you?'

'Being bullied and hassled was never going to happen to me again. When you first get to a prison they take you into Reception and then they allocate you on to a wing. You soon become aware that the jail is run to a pecking order.'

'Different types of people?'

'How weak or strong you are.' Roy grimaced. 'There are the scumbags and outcasts – the child molesters or rapists – nobody wants to be associated with them.'

'They have a hard time in prison.'

'They deserve it,' Roy growled. 'Next up the ladder are the run-of-the-mill prisoners, the mediocre ones, petty thieves and two-bob merchants. They're not scumbags, they're not tough guys, they're not anybody. In fact, they're totally insignificant.' Roy drank what was left of his coffee and I refilled it for him. He went on. 'Then there is the hierarchy – the guv'nors. These are the tough guys, the men who actually run the prison. They are murderers, bank robbers and gangsters.'

I shivered. 'Where did you fit in?'

'I was certainly not a scumbag and there's no way I was insignificant. Although I was young at the time, I somehow fitted in with the big boys and they accepted me. They took to me. I wasn't frightened of anyone and they recognised this in me. I was one of their own, one of the chaps.'

'Did you soon settle down?'

'I had to. I was in the prison routine and I accepted my lot. I wouldn't take any shit from anybody.'

'Was it in Maidstone where you were in the riot?'

Roy smiled. 'Riot! It was more like a fucking comic opera.'

'What happened?'

'One of the screws started it.'

'Why was that?'

'I wasn't doing what they wanted. The doctor was there to see me and he told me to stick my tongue out. So I told him to fuck off.'

'I bet that went down well.'

'If they'd had any sense they'd have left it. I didn't need the doctor hassling me. They should have just let it go. But they have such drab little lives, they like their bit of power ... you had to toe the line and jump to it or else they went for you. This one made a big mistake. Instead of thinking, Well, if Shaw doesn't want to see the doctor, it's his decision, he went mad and punched me in the gut. It was totally unnecessary. He winded me and I flipped. I felt an adrenalin rush through my body. I told him, "You shouldn't have fucking done that," and I grabbed him by the collar and nutted him. He fell out of the cell.'

'What did he do?'

'He slammed the door shut in my face and I wasn't gonna take that. I was raging, bursting with fury. How dare he fucking hit me? Who the fuck does he think he is? What the fuck did I do? I could hear them outside and I started screaming at them.' Roy's face had reddened and his eyes were blazing as he relived the moment. '"When I come out of here, you'll be sorry. I'm coming after you and hell's coming with me." I kept yelling and kicking the cell door. I was telling them what I thought of them.'

'What was that?'

'Fucking slags. Nobody took any notice of me. I kept kicking the door and creating a racket and they blanked me.'

'They thought you were going to give in.'

'They were wrong. I started smashing up the furniture. There was a big heavy chair and I flung it at the wall and it smashed into pieces. I grabbed the seat and started bashing the spy hole in the door. I was like a madman. The adrenalin rush made me so mad I felt I could knock down a castle. I had a burning obsession to get that door open and get out of there.'

'They were keen to keep you inside.'

Roy nodded. 'They knew they'd started a fire they couldn't put out.'

'Did you run out of steam?'

'Did I hell!' he snarled. 'I hit the door with such an almighty crash that I felt it starting to cave in. The metal supports were going. The glass on the spy hole broke. I clobbered that door so hard the metal started to split. And then I did it. It gave way and there was a hole just big enough for me to climb through.'

'That was when they disappeared.'

Roy grinned. 'I ran along the landing ... it was totally deserted. The screws were nowhere to be seen. The other cons were all locked up, they were hollering and screaming with delight.'

'Because you were out?'

'Because I'd got one over on the system.'

'What did you do? Did you think you could get outside of the prison? Escape?'

'I wasn't thinking that far ahead. It was a feeling of elation just to get out of that cell. I ran downstairs, no one tried to stop me. A pal of mine called Freddie Samson was in an observation cell. He was worried for me. He told me to get back in my cell or I'd get into trouble.'

'What did you say to him?'

'I laughed. I told him I'd just ripped the fucking door off my cell. Freddie could see out of the window, his cell overlooked the main gate. He could see that the screws were getting ready to storm the wing.'

'Battle stations.' The image of Roy, as a young man, holding Maidstone Prison to ransom was totally unreal. How had a visit from the doc turned into a full-scale riot?

'Freddie told me they had riot shields, truncheons and even dogs. He kept pleading with me to give myself up.'

'Did you consider it?'

Roy's eyes met mine. 'Not for a minute. I was pumping, nothing could have stopped me. This was war. I went to the top of the landing and sorted out my defences. I positioned all the fire buckets round the top of the stairs. Some were full of sand, some water. It was all going over the screws when they came for me.'

'Like a medieval siege.' I thought it was lucky he didn't have boiling oil to hand. 'Did they come and get you?'

'They tried. The riot squad came on to the wing mob-handed. They hadn't a clue what situation they were walking into. I peered over the steel girders and waited. When they came into the right position, I poured the sand and water over them and, just for good measure, I threw the buckets at them, too. It was like Brighton beach.'

'Sand and water everywhere.' It sounded horribly funny.

Roy smiled, although the smile didn't reach his eyes. 'The riot squad were slipping and sliding everywhere. Falling over each other. A few of them managed to scramble up the stairs and they started running after me.'

'What did you do?'

'Without thinking, I ran one way and they followed. The chair leg was still in my hand. I was hanging on to it. It was my only weapon. I came to the end of the landing. I was cornered, so I stopped and turned and gave a great yell. A cry of defiance and I ran straight at them waving my chair leg.'

'They must have been terrified.'

'They turned on their heels and ran back down that landing. Then they thought about what plonkers they were and turned and chased me again. It was like a scene from the Keystone Cops.'

'What was happening in the rest of the prison?'

'It was bedlam. Prisoners were banging on their cells doors. They were shouting and chanting: "LEAVE ... HIM ... ALONE, LEAVE ... HIM ... ALONE." It was absolute mayhem. They weren't taking any notice of the screws. Nobody could shut them up.'

'It was turning into a full-scale crisis.'

'That was what they thought.'

'So what did they do?'

'They fetched the Governor. It was unheard of to get him out at 10.30 at night but anyway he came. He stood on the landing in the middle of all this chaos. Then he shouted at the top of his voice, "SHAW, STOP THIS NONSENSE NOW." Everything went suddenly quiet. They all stopped what they were doing.

'He had a very loud, deep voice and he shouted again.

"IF YOU COME DOWN, I WILL DEAL WITH YOU PERSONALLY IN THE MORNING." '

'What did that mean?'

'It was the best outcome for me. I knew that I would only get another 14 days on my sentence. That was as much as the Governor's powers would permit. I weighed it up.'

'Had you cooled down a bit by then?'

'There was that. If I went on with it, I knew I would get another six months. So, I shouted to the other prisoners: "DID YOU HEAR THAT EVERYBODY?"

'And they all shouted back. "YEAH, WE HEARD IT, ROY."

'And it was all over?'

'Yes. I did 14 days in the punishment block. The Governor was true to his word. They shipped me off to Canterbury Prison. But they couldn't handle me there. Almost straight away they sent me to Pentonville.'

'What was that like?'

'I met three of the most feared men in the prison system – Mad Frankie Fraser, Jimmy Andrews and Jimmy Essex.' Roy's eyes met mine, they were hostile and unnerving in their intensity. 'Do you judge a man by the company he keeps?' he asked me.

I nodded. 'Some people do,' I told him.

'Well, you could say that I was in good company,' he said reflectively. 'Make no mistake, they were ruthless men.'

Roy stood up suddenly and told me he was going to his car. He had left his mobile in the glove box and needed to check his calls. It was hard to know what he felt about the vicious men he met in prison. Did he see the mirror image of himself? I couldn't imagine that he would fear even the worst killer. Did he look at them and see himself – there but for the grace of God go I? Or did he think he was different, that he was treading a different path?

The sun had gone in and I moved the chairs back indoors. When he came back, I intended to do my best to find out.

CHAPTER 17

GOOD COMPANY

AFTER LUNCH, ROY BEGAN TELLING ME ABOUT
LIFE IN PENTONVILLE.

'Why were Frankie Fraser, Jimmy Andrews and Jimmy
Essex so feared?' These blokes would have put the fear of
God in anyone but, to have this reputation within the
prison population, they had to be especially dangerous.

'It wasn't because they were big muscle men. They were
ordinary-looking men. If you left them alone, showed
them respect, you were OK, but if you were foolish enough
to fuck with them, it would only be a matter of time before
they came back to cut your throat. Make no mistake about
it, if you pissed them off they'd do you.'

'Did you hear about this happening?'

Roy nodded. 'Hear about it? I saw it myself. I was in the
dinner queue at Pentonville and this was the highlight of

the day. Even though the food was crap, we were hungry. I collected my tin tray and I stood there, moaning with everybody else. Jimmy Essex was in the line next to me. Another con elbowed his way in front of Jimmy as if he were invisible. No "Please", no "Do you mind?", no "Sorry".

'Well, Jimmy got the needle. He tapped the geezer on the shoulder and motioned with his thumb to get back. The bloke turned to look at him. I suppose that Jimmy didn't look as though he posed much of a threat.'

'What did he look like?'

'Average. Small, middle-aged with a bald head and glasses. This stupid con looked Jimmy up and down and said to him, "Go away, you old plonker."

'I looked at Jimmy, he just glared at the geezer and smiled. "An old plonker, am I?" he said.

'Straight away he puts his dinner tray down and goes back to his cell to collect a sock. When he returned to the queue, he winked at me and tapped the geezer on the shoulder again. "An old plonker, am I?" he says. Then he hit the man so hard in the face that he knocked him sparko.'

'Was it something in the sock?'

Roy nodded. 'Yes, he'd put a salt pot in it. The man's face was bust open. A mess.' He paused reflectively. 'That was how it was. A row over a place in the dinner queue.'

'You were all on a short fuse.'

'Men always are in prison. I've known fellas who've gone inside on a two-year stretch and never come out again. They've lost their rag over something or other, done what they shouldn't have – it's a slippery slope when you're doing time. There's no second chances. Look at Charlie Bronson, he's a case in point.'

I agreed. Charlie had misbehaved and his violent nature gained him more and more time inside. 'What happened to Jimmy in the end?'

'He never got done for bashing the geezer up. Nobody was ever going to point the finger. They knew what would happen if they did. He wasn't a man to fight fair and square, he's a man who picked his moment. Caught them off guard.'

'Dangerous.'

'Very,' Roy agreed.

'Later, I heard that Jimmy Essex was found guilty of murder while he was still in prison. It didn't surprise me; he was a man whose dignity far outweighed his principles.'

'What about the other two?'

'Jimmy Andrews was a proud man. A man of honour, but unfortunately he was shot dead soon after his release.'

'And Mad Frankie Fraser?'

'He was in the Richardson gang. In the '60s, London was dominated by two main gangs – the Krays and the Richardsons. It's been said they terrorized the communities in which they lived. Well, Frankie was with the Richardsons. They'd all grown up together. He was doing seven years for cutting Jack Spot. I don't know how long he's done inside all together.'

'A lot.' I'd heard that he'd done 40 years in total.

'Me and Frankie crossed paths quite a few times. He

lived up to his name. He told me that they had the cellars in their offices done up as cells. When they wanted to persuade anyone to talk to them, they used to show them the cellar and say, "Which one do you want to die in? The left or the right?" It always worked.'

'He was in a gang, but you were never part of that?'

Roy shook his head. 'I worked on my own. That suited me.'

'Did you have any regrets?'

'No. I'm sure Frankie would say the same, the only thing we regretted was getting caught.' Roy looked down at his hands. 'But you know, prison is one huge cesspit. I would never recommend it to anyone. It's not big and it's not clever to go to prison, it's a complete waste of a human life. All the men who society can no longer tolerate are dumped there. It's like a huge holding tank full of misery. All the murderers, the armed robbers, the thieves and cut-throats are contained in one big building. They've been denied their liberty by the law. That's one thing. Then they're denied their fundamental rights as human beings. They don't have any dignity, it's stripped away from them, even the right to use the toilet. It's like a melting pot of evil, a male-dominated world where prisoners are thrust with no means of escape. Everything gets out of proportion, there are riots over the slightest thing.'

Roy was jabbing at the air with his finger. It was strange to see that, in this at least, he is on the side of the experts who say that prison doesn't work.

'What you have to realise is that in any pack of animals

there is only one dominant male. So what we have in prison is that all these dominant males have been taken away from their packs and confined together for months and years at a time. It's a recipe for disaster.'

'It sounds terrifying and dangerous.'

Roy nodded. 'Believe me, Katie, it is. There is not a single man in there who doesn't have problems. They all have to deal with them somehow. It increases the tension. More than a few of the geezers will be tinged with madness. They're unpredictable. Bang them all up together and what have you got? An extremely dangerous house on the hill that's waiting to explode – a disaster in the making. These men have nothing to lose and everything to prove.'

'And everybody has their own cross to bear.'

Roy agreed. 'They're heavier inside.'

'Have you been able to forget a grudge?'

Roy gave me a scornful look. 'No. I think you know that by now.'

I'd heard the rumours; would Roy tell me how far he'd gone in settling scores? 'What about Albert Rainbird ... wasn't he a mate of yours?'

Roy's face darkened. 'I'm loath to say it, but he used to be a friend. I'd have considered him a good friend at one time. We used to work together.'

'Work, as in ...'

'Doing robberies. We served time together, we'd look out for one another.'

'What sort of a man was he in those days?'

Roy smiled. 'He liked a row. He wasn't afraid of having

a tear-up. But most of all he liked to see me in a row. Metaphorically speaking, he'd load the gun and I'd fire the bullets.'

'So what went wrong?'

'I began to hear things about him on the grapevine. That he'd turned bad, that he was a wrong 'un. At first I didn't believe it, I'd considered him a friend. Then I found out that he'd grassed a mate up. It really knocked me back. How could he do that? I'd got him sussed out all wrong, so I started delving a bit deeper. I had the feeling that he'd started living on immoral earnings, getting young girls on the vice game. In my book, that made him a no-good pimp. He'd turned out to be a right old mongrel.'

'And then he arrived at the same prison as you?'

'We were in Parkhurst together. I decided that his number was up, he'd played his games long enough. I decided to hurt him and hurt him bad. He was going to look in the mirror every morning and have something to remember me by. You need a blade or a piece of glass to hurt somebody – the only thing I had was my hair cream bottle.'

'What did you do?'

'I smashed the bottle and got myself a good piece and I sharpened it on the stone windowsill until it was like a razor. When we were allowed out for exercise I slipped my makeshift knife into my donkey jacket pocket and I was set. I looked out for Rainbird and then I spotted him. I couldn't take my eyes off him, he was laughing and chatting with a screw. He hadn't a clue what was coming.

It made me madder than ever to see him. Talking to a screw? Nobody does that unless they're a no-good grass.'

'Weren't you bothered about anybody seeing you?'

Roy shook his head. 'What were they going to do to me? Send me to prison? Anyway, I had to pick my moment; there was plenty of activity in the yard, lots of eyes and ears. I waited until the whistle blew for us to go back inside. It was the end of the recreation period. All the prisoners filed back in line. I made my way through the pack until I was right behind Rainbird.

'He was finishing a smoke. He took a last drag and then dropped the ciggie on to the floor and ground it in with his foot. It was my chance. While everybody was milling about I grabbed him by the neck and forced his head back.

His mouth came open but he never made a sound, he knew it was me and he had a look of shock and disbelief on his face. I took out my makeshift razor and I dragged it straight across his throat. It only took a second. I screamed at him, "TAKE A LOOK AT MY FACE, RAINBIRD. THIS IS THE LAST THING YOU'RE EVER GONNA SEE."

'He let out a blood-curdling yell and clutched his throat, blood was spurting through his hands and he was rasping for breath, making a sort of gurgling sound. I could see that he was trying to call for help but it was too late. He couldn't get the words out. He tried to gasp for breath but there was no air. His eyes bulged with fear and panic. Then I punched him and down he went.'

'Did they all see what you did?' It was a horrific scenario.

'It was a mêlée. The guards knew something was up,

they'd heard his first yell. People were running about, they didn't have a clue who'd done it. They were blowing whistles, all they could think about was getting us back on to the wing and a lock down.'

'Was he dead?' I whispered.

Roy shrugged. 'I didn't give a fuck if he was dead or not. I saw them cart him off to hospital.'

'Did he make it?'

'Yeah.' The disappointment was written all over Roy's face. 'The doctors saved his life. Only just. In my opinion, he wasn't worth saving, he was a dirty mongrel, a throwback, he should have been drowned at birth.'

'Didn't you get into any trouble for it?'

'Nobody said a word. When I was in Pentonville with Fraser, Essex and Andrews, I got into all sorts of trouble. We all did. I was full of rage at everyone and everything. I was so furious with society, I lashed out at every opportunity – screws, nonces, grasses, you name it, I did them all.'

'What about child molesters?'

Roy's face had a savage expression. 'I took most pleasure in hurting them. The authorities knew what was going on but they didn't have any evidence. All they could see was a violent young man. We got into so much trouble that at one stage the Home Office stamped on our records: "SHAW AND FRASER MUST NEVER BE IN THE SAME PRISON AGAIN".'

I glanced at my watch and excused myself, it was time to decide the next day's menus with the chef. Roy was settled by the fire, a drink in his hand. So far, he'd been in a good frame of mind, the mood to talk. It's always an emotional experience going back over past ground, the highs and lows, mistakes and disappointments. Roy's life had been more intense than most. There was so much I still wanted to know. What happened when he met Jack 'The Hat' ... Frank the Mad Axeman ... George Cornell ...?

I looked through the open doorway. Roy was staring into the fire, thinking or brooding. He seemed to have enjoyed telling me everything so far, but it's hard to know his real emotions. Perhaps it was time for some comfort food. I decided to make a pot of tea, cut some thick ham and mustard sandwiches and then I was going back inside to take a chance and rattle his cage some more.

CHAPTER 18

ONLY THE LONELY
PART ONE

ROY HAD LEFT SOON AFTER OUR CONVERSATION ABOUT PRISON. He said he had to get back home to take his dogs out. There was a boxing show in aid of a children's charity later on and he was booked to attend. He'd arranged to meet one of his young lady friends afterwards. They would be going for a meal and then on to a nightclub. Roy has a busy life, but ... I still had the feeling that something was missing, even though he didn't care to admit it.

I was resolved to find his Dorothy if I possibly could. I went back to the housing estate to see the elderly lady in the bungalow later in the week.

Over a cup of tea and a chat in her cosy sitting room, she remembered a lot more about her former neighbour. It did sound like the Dorothy Tyler I was looking for; she wasn't married, she'd doted on her Rottweiler and she'd taken her dog with her when she left.

I said my goodbyes and thank yous and eventually managed to get away. I was on the case now and it was on to the next clue. If she'd had a dog, she must have been registered with a vet.

I did a tour of all the local pet care centres and found that Dorothy had been registered with the veterinary surgeon on the High Street. They were a bit reluctant to give me the information at first. It might breach their commitment to confidentiality and why did I want to know? I made the usual explanations and eventually they conceded that the Pet Police wouldn't call round to arrest them and the sky wouldn't fall in if they checked their records for a D Tyler.

The girl looked methodically through the cards. Yes, Dorothy Tyler. It was the address I'd been to and she did have a Rottweiler. But ... she was no longer a client. Damn it. I'd hoped that Dorothy might still be living locally. I'd come so far, though, and I wasn't going to be beaten. Is there a forwarding address? Where is she now?

It was like winkling a cockle out of its shell, but in the end I dragged it out of them. They'd sent her dog's records to a vet in Sheffield. Yes! I was a step nearer.

I planned to visit the steel city as soon as possible.

I didn't feel as though I could face Roy again without having something to tell him so I put off meeting him for a couple of weeks. I decided to look up an old friend of his on the way up north and, as I needed a visiting order to get in to see him, I had to wait a week 'til the arrangements were all in place. This wasn't your average geezer in jail nor an ordinary VO. I was going to see one of the most dangerous prisoners in the penal system and an old pal of Roy's – Charles Bronson.

Woodhill Prison in Milton Keynes is a top-security prison with a special unit designed for men with no release date and nothing to lose. It's a prison within a prison, known as Britain's Alcatraz. Charlie has spent 24 years out of the last 28 in solitary confinement in prisons like Woodhill.

It's been a lonley life. He's been locked in dungeons, in iron boxes concreted into the middle of cells and has endured more periods of isolation than any other living British prisoner. He has even, famously, been locked into a cage like the fictional Hannibal Lecter.

Charlie has spent months at a time with nothing more than the cockroaches for company. He is always held under maximum security, in a Spartan cell with little more than a fire-proof bed and a table and chair made from compressed cardboard. When his cell is unlocked, there are up to 12 prison officers, sometimes in riot gear and with dogs, standing by.

I arrived for my visit half-an-hour early. I parked my car and went to the reception desk, told them my name and gave them my passport for identification.

Most visitors to prison go into a communal reception and wait their turn to be called into the visiting room in the main prison block. But I was shown into a small secure room. An officer handed me a piece of paper with a number on it and motioned his head towards a large tray. I was told to remove my jacket, shoes and watch ready to be searched. I passed through an x-ray machine identical to the ones you find at airports. I was then asked to move to another area and stand on a special box with both my arms out in order to be frisked.

I was told to open my mouth and lift my tongue. An officer looked in my ears and up my nose, then felt under my arms and around my chest and down my body.

I couldn't decide whether it felt more like an army medical or a scene from a B-rated gangster movie. I had to lift my feet so that they could examine in between my toes. I was then told to lean back and throw my hair forward. I asked what they were looking for – it was concealed drugs and weapons.

Eventually, I was given back the tray containing my possessions and permission was granted for me to continue to the next gate. They weren't taking any chances and I was accompanied by three officers.

'Lima two six, lima two six, permission to walk?' whispered one of the officers into a small radio. Each step of the way was the same.

We went through one gate and then had to wait until permission was granted for us to move on to the next. In the final reception area, I was searched for the second time. The only thing I was allowed to take into the inner sanctums of the prison was a bag of loose change for the vending machines.

Charlie had left a list for me; he wanted six chocolate bars and four bottles of Buxton spring water.

The vending machines were difficult to figure out; the first one didn't work, it swallowed my coins and then ignored me. The next was geared up for crisps and cups of teas, it was out of choc bars. It was taking such a long time. An officer came in and said that Charlie was getting agitated, he didn't like to be kept waiting. He told me to go in and they'd sort the shopping list out for me later.

I continued my journey through the prison, conscious of the swivelling eyes of the surveillance cameras following my every move.

The silence was eerie and only broken by the sound of jangling keys and squeaky boots on polished floors. Eventually, two male officers opened a door and showed me into a small room furnished with two long tables. One had a single chair one side and three chairs on the other.

Already sitting at the other table were four prison officers. They stood up as Charlie was brought in. If I'd expected drab prison strides, I was mistaken. Charlie likes to make a fashion statement and he didn't disappoint; he was wearing a chequered pea green and canary yellow boiler suit. He had a shaven head and a beard down to his navel – oh, and little round sunglasses like John Lennon used to wear.

Charlie smiled and so did I. He looked at me with a puzzled expression. I thought of ways to start the conversation but he kicked off first.

'Are they your real teeth?' he asked me in a gruff voice. As opening gambits go, it was certainly different.

'Yes,' I told him with a big smile.

Charlie walked towards me and I could see the officers tense.

'Can I tap 'em?' he asked.

I exposed all my pearly gates and, gently with his finger, he proceeded to tap my teeth one by one.

'Ooh, lovely,' he cooed. 'Come on, sit down, let's have a chat.'

As the six officers, Charlie Bronson and myself sat down in the small, cramped room, I felt relieved. I asked him a few routine questions to break the ice.

'When were you born, Charlie?'

'Sixth of December 1951,' he told me.

'You're under the birth sign of Sagittarius then.'

Charlie smiled. 'Is that good, Kate?'

I didn't know whether it was or not. 'Do you have any brothers or sisters?'

He nodded. 'Two brothers, John and Mark.'

'Did you have a happy childhood?'

'It was mad.' He paused and fingered his beard. 'That's my most dangerous weapon.'

I didn't quite follow.

'My madness and unpredictability,' he said with all seriousness. I flicked a glance at the prison officers, they shifted uncomfortably. Charlie went on, 'My problem is that I just change in a spin and become something that's not human.' He looked directly at me.

'I'm not really a wicked man, but put an axe in my hand and I'll show you an abattoir.'

My mouth felt dry. 'What's your toughest moment?' I managed to stutter.

He thought for a moment or two. 'Holding a guy by his feet from a balcony 18 floors up and deciding whether to let go.'

'Did you?' The thought flashed into my mind that, no matter what Charlie does, they can't punish him any further.

He shook his head. 'No, I pulled him in. I regret it now.'

'You're sorry you didn't kill him?'

'Yes, the man's a rat. Maybe next time.'

I wondered if the threat of the final deterrent would have changed his attitude? Would capital punishment have made any difference to Charlie Bronson's behaviour?

'Do you believe in hanging?' I asked him.

Surprisingly Charlie does, although not, of course, for him. 'Yes, all paedophiles should hang. There is no cure for them. Kids are innocent and scum who kill them should be hung.' This is a popular belief in prison.

'You've met a lot of tough men over the years. What about Roy Shaw? How do you rate him?'

Charlie smiled. 'Roy is a great guy. As tough as they come. Not any ordinary tough guy, there's lots of them in here, Roy's different. He's a warrior.'

That was a good way to describe him. 'When did you last meet him?'

'It was at my trial in Luton in February 2000. He's a

good mate and he came to show his solid support. I appreciated it, especially as there was a "traitor" in the public gallery.'

'What do you mean?'

'A spy, a bastard.'

'Someone who's crossed you in the past?'

Charlie nodded. 'Yes, but Roy soon saw him off.'

'What did he do?'

'He didn't have to do anything much, he's Roy Shaw. People respect him. They know what's coming if they don't.' Charlie gave a deep belly laugh. 'Roy only had to give him a stern look and the bloke left promptly.'

'Did you ever see Roy fight?'

'Yes, I've seen him. He could have been one of the greatest heavyweight boxers of all time.'

'How does he compare to other boxers?'

'Roy was like Frazier and Marciano, he just kept coming at you. When you watch the likes of some of the others, they're like fairies. No comparison.'

'You've done some unlicensed boxing yourself, haven't you?'

Charlie's eyes lit up. 'When I was on the fight scene, I put out a challenge to Lenny McLean. And I was ready for him. I was just out of jail after 14 long, hard years. I was hungry for a fight. I felt as though I was going to explode. I needed to let off steam. I had three fights in 60 days and won them all.'

'What about Lenny?'

Charlie shook his head. 'He never took up my

challenge. Maybe it was because he was so nice and comfortable by then.'

'He was settled down?'

'Yes. We tried all ways, my manager Paul Edmunds put down "winner takes all" to try to tempt him, but it was no joy.'

'What did you do next?'

Charlie shrugged. 'Nothing for me to do – I went back on to the pavement with my shooter – a man's gotta eat, a man's gotta live.'

I glanced at the prison officers, their eyes were flicking round the room; Charlie had caught them out before, now they were constantly watchful.

'How long were you outside?'

Charlie adjusted his sunglasses. 'Sixty-nine days of freedom, then it was back to jail.'

'Do you think prison is a deterrent?'

He shook his head. 'No way. How could it be? Prison just breeds tougher villains.'

That was exactly what Roy had said. 'Would anything have deterred you from a life of crime?'

Charlie grinned. 'Love, understanding and apple pies,' he told me. 'If you're a tough guy, you need to have feelings and a sense of fairness.'

'What about Roy? Does he have that?'

'Without a doubt. Roy has respect. He doesn't mess about.'

'Would you trust him?'

'Yes, I would. It's a hard thing to come by these days,

but if Roy gave you his word, that would be it. He'd stick by it no matter what.'

'A bad enemy,' I murmured.

'He goes to the finish,' Charlie agreed. 'He doesn't let anyone step over the mark.'

'You've known him a long time?'

'We were both in Broadmoor.' Charlie gave a short laugh. 'It's for the criminally insane. It's a lonely place. All prison is lonely. Basically, it's down to you. You either survive it or you don't. I nearly killed a man while I was at Broadmoor.'

'How did that come about?'

'My mum and dad had just been to see me. Basically, I was feeling happy, then this bloke spoiled it for me. We lived in dormitories at that time and we'd crossed paths before. Then I found out they'd put this guy called Gordon Robinson in the next bed to me.'

'That was asking for trouble.'

'I knew our paths would cross one day. I went back to the ward from my visit and there he was, with his key in my locker. The toe-rag was trying to open it.'

'A locker thief?' That wouldn't go down well. Prison rule number one – do not steal from other cons.

'Yes. I hauled him away and then I chinned him. But it wasn't enough for me. I wanted to kill him. I felt as though he deserved to die.'

'Because he tried to break into your locker?'

Charlie's eyes narrowed and I saw one of the prison officers give me a warning look.

Charlie went on with his tale. 'My dad had given me a favourite tie a few years earlier. It was my favourite tie. I locked myself in the toilet and tested its strength on the cistern. It was strong all right. It held my weight.'

'What did you want the tie for?'

'I'd decided to strangle the bloke that night. I felt excited. Just thinking about it gave me a buzz. It was the same buzz I got from doing armed robberies.'

I thought about this. Roy had said the same, he'd told me how hyped up he felt when he was waiting to start a job. I began to wonder if this is all crime is about – that and money! Are these men just adrenalin junkies?

I decided the time wasn't right to put that point to Charlie. I sat still and quiet and waited for him to go on.

'I walked into the dormitories with the tie round my waist under my pyjamas out of sight. I climbed into bed and waited. I could see Robinson huddling down under the covers, his left eye was closed from where I'd hit him earlier, but his other eye was alert. I smiled at him. My best smile.'

That might be when he's most dangerous. The thought went buzzing through my head. Charlie's face was bright and lively, smiling at the memories. Crocodiles look as though they're smiling, don't they? Then they grab you and kill you. My hands were clammy, but I knew I was safe with Charlie, he would never hurt a woman.

Charlie went on. 'The night nurse looked in every half-hour or so through the observation slit in the door. I only needed a couple of minutes. Fuck the night watchman!

There was no saving the thief. I lay still, deep in thought, the tie wrapped round my waist, just waiting. Like a spider waits for a fly. Time was plentiful, I had all night long. This was my night, my fly, I was buzzing. Twelve o'clock, one o'clock, I waited patiently, watching every bed, every movement.

'Then it happened, as if I'd sent the thief a telegraphic message. He moved. He sat up. He bent over to put his slippers on. He was probably going for a piss.'

'What did you do?'

'I leapt out of bed and in a second the tie was wrapped round his scrawny neck. I was strangling the locker thief.' Charlie's hands were clenched. In his mind he was still doing it. 'It felt magic. It felt right.'

'Didn't he call out?'

'No. Surprisingly there was very little noise. A sigh, a groan at first, but then nothing. I pulled tighter and leaned over to watch. His eyes bulged, his face went grey, his tongue protruded. Dribble ran from the corner of his mouth. He pissed himself, I smelt shit.'

'He was dying.' I tried not to let Charlie see me shudder.

'Yes. He was on his way out of planet earth. Then it happened. The tie snapped. I had half the tie in one hand and half in the other. He began making noises, animal grunts and deep chesty moans. Other patients were waking up. I had to act fast. I was in trouble.'

'What did you do?'

'I punched him in the face and straddled over his bed. I shouted to the loons that he was having a nightmare.'

'You were trying to make them think you were reviving him?'

'It didn't work. The purple welts round his neck told their own story.'

'What did they do to you?'

Charlie shrugged. 'I spent the next four years in Broadmoor's hell hole – the punishment blocks.'

'Roy has spent time in there.'

'Yeah, I know. They try to break you.'

'Did you ever fight Roy?'

Charlie shook his head. 'No, I've too much respect for the man for that. He's a friend and mainly I wouldn't fight him because he's the true Guv'nor. Our era's more than two decades apart and it's not for me to step up into such a man's era. He's earned his titles. Blood, sweat and more blood.'

I saw the prison officers shuffling, looking at their watches and pushing their chairs back. It was nearly time to go.

Charlie turned to look at them. 'Is that it?' he asked them.

'Time to go, Charlie,' they told him.

'Another minute,' I pleaded. There was one more thing I wanted to ask Charlie. 'Is there anything you know about Roy that no one else knows? Something like a secret?'

His eyes narrowed.

'Nothing he wouldn't want you to tell me,' I reassured him. 'You've known him for years, isn't there anything?'

Charlie shook his head. 'I dunno. The man's an icon and

I salute him. I've fought with him, I've fought for him but I've never fought against him. There is ...' He hesitated. 'I don't know how to put this, Kate,' he told me with a roguish grin.

'Go on,' I said.

'Well, I know he has a reputation as a ladies' man. I'd say it's well deserved.'

'What do you mean?'

'Finish your visit,' the prison officer said in a stern voice. Charlie got up straight away. There is little doubt that prison indoctrinates and institutionalises long-term inmates. Before he left, Charlie leaned towards me. All six prison officers took a step forward. I lifted my hand, I was all right. He bent to whisper in my ear. 'The only secret I know is ... and I don't think he'd mind me telling you.' I felt Charlie's hot breath whisper in my shell-like ... I felt my face colour up. Charlie turned to go. 'There won't ever be another Roy Shaw,' he called out. 'You'd better believe it.'

Poor old Charlie Bronson, I thought, as they led him away and the metal door clanged shut behind him.

CHAPTER 19

ON THE TRAIL

THE VET IN SHEFFIELD WASN'T HARD TO FIND. Manor Pet Care Centre was a large, upmarket surgery in a posh district. I rang the polished brass bell and almost immediately there was a low buzzing noise and a disembodied voice said, 'Please enter.' I walked down a well-polished, oak-floored corridor and opened the door into a room marked 'Reception'. There were flowers on the desk, magazines on the table and Vivaldi playing in a constant loop in the background – but the room was empty. Only the slightest smell of disinfectant, a wall chart showing highly coloured and very scary parasitic worms and a faint yapping in the background gave away the fact that this was a doggy hospital and not Harley Street. I wondered where all the customers were. After a few minutes, the door opened and a 20-something receptionist bustled in.

'I'm sorry to keep you waiting,' she said with a fixed smile.

After my style and fashion tutorials at Harrods, I was aware that she was dressed smart/casual. Her hair was smooth, super glossy and well cut, the shoes said Prada and the discreet jewellery made an expensive chic statement that even the austere green medico jacket didn't diminish.

'How can I help you?' she asked in a slightly patronising tone. I realised that I should have brought a sick ferret with me just to break the ice; maybe she thought I was a rep and going to try to sell her something.

'It's a bit quiet today, isn't it?' I looked round at the empty chairs.

'We have an appointment system,' she told me, looking at her watch. 'It usually works very well.'

I took the hint and began to explain the reason for my visit.

'I'm afraid we can't disclose any information about our clients,' she told me sniffily.

'You're not even able to tell me if Dorothy Tyler is a client?'

She shook her head.

I did my best to persuade her but she there was no way this tough cookie was going to spill the beans. I turned to go, feeling dispirited. Another brick wall. Then I had an inspired thought.

'Can I make an appointment to see the vet?' She looked disappointed and suspicious as to my motives, but reluctantly she fitted me in for 11.00am. I had a hunch that when I got past the dragon lady, the boss man might be easier to deal with.

I went for a walk in the nearby park, had an ice cream and watched the ducks on the pond until it was time to go back. The vet was much easier to get on with.

'Come in, come in ...' He ushered me into a dazzling white surgery. 'Have you left your dog in the car?' he said, rubbing his hands.

I was sorry to disappoint him, but I explained the reason for my visit. He was easy to talk to and I told him almost everything – about Roy, Dorothy, long-lost love, hard times, the elderly neighbour and the Rottweiler dog. 'So you see, you're my last hope.'

After the response from the receptionist I didn't know what to expect. But the vet was a 'friends reunited' addict and a romantic at heart.

'Well, I'm sure ... I don't see what harm it could do ... if it gets them back together ... in the circumstances ... let's have a look.' He began flicking through the folders in his filing cabinet.

'Yes,' he said. 'Here we are.' He lifted out a slim buff file. 'Dorothy Tyler and Connie and King Tyler.'

'Connie and King?'

'Two Rottweilers,' he told me. 'An adult male and a six-month-old bitch puppy.'

So Dorothy had acquired another dog.

'And her address? I know you shouldn't but ... I only want to tell her that Roy is desperate to see her again. If she doesn't want to see him, that's it. It's up to her.'

The vet shook his head.

'I'm sorry, I can't help you.' My disappointment must have showed on my face. 'No, it's not that I won't,' he said hastily. 'I can't. We don't know where she is. She had a temporary address with us. It was the place where she worked – a leisure centre in the Peak District. A new venture, it belongs to a pal of mine, actually. Lakes, cycling trails. Good fun.'

It sounded it.

'She isn't there now though,' he added.

'How do you know?'

'Because Connie was having a course of treatment for a skin allergy and we tried to get in touch with Mrs Tyler. There was something new we could have tried. But she'd moved away.'

'Given her job up?'

'Yes. Some domestic problems they said. Perhaps she found it hard to settle. She's a Londoner, isn't she?'

'You don't have any idea where she is?'

He shook his head. 'The dog's records are still here. So she can't have gone to another vet.'

I thanked him and turned to go.

This seemed like yet another dead end. What now?

'Hold on a moment,' the vet called out as I reached the door. 'I've just thought of something her employer said.'

'What was that?'

'That it was sad that Mrs Tyler had to give the dogs up. She was devoted to them but wherever she was going she couldn't take them with her. She was looking for a new home for them.'

'I see. What did she do? She didn't ...' I love dogs and I couldn't bear to think that she'd had them put down.

'Oh no.' He shook his head. 'I'd have known that straight away.' He put Dorothy's file back in the cabinet and began looking through a notebook. 'I think she was very upset at getting rid of them,' he said absent-mindedly.

'What did she do then?' I asked.

'Here we are.' He beamed and handed me a card. 'This is what you're looking for. This is where she took Connie and King.'

I read the words 'St Bernard's Animal Sanctuary'. It was a home for rescued animals at Chesterfield. There was a phone number, an address, a website.

I thanked the vet and left feeling my spirits rise. I was back on the trail. But if the dogs were in the local pound, what on earth had happened to Dorothy?

I rang Roy on my mobile phone and brought him up to speed.

'What do you think I should do?'

'Get round there straight away. Fetch the dogs out with you. I don't care what it takes. I'll have them, bring them down here,' he growled. 'Why the hell didn't she come to me if she was in trouble?'

I smiled to myself. Aren't men strange? They'd split up years ago and he still thinks she ought to come running to him if things aren't going right.

It was because in the past they'd meant such a lot to each other. So why hadn't Dorothy done this? Perhaps she thought he didn't care after all this time. I just had to get these two back and talking to each other again.

'You know, they might still not be around ... that's to say ...' I tried to prepare him for the unthinkable. 'These dog rescue centres aren't always able to keep unwanted pets. They have a cut-off date and then ...'

Roy didn't want to think about this. He's a great dog lover and Rottweilers are his favourite breed. But I wasn't so sure. Big dogs. Expensive to feed. Perhaps difficult to re-home. Would they still be there? Maybe we were too late.

'I'll go round there right away,' I told him and promised to ring him as soon as there was any news.

A lot of different scenarios were running through my head as I drove to the animal sanctuary. What if the dogs were dead? Dorothy must have been at a low ebb if this had happened. What if they'd been re-homed? Would they still tell me where Dorothy is? What if they were still there?

I guessed I'd be driving back to London with two Rotties in the back seat.

The sanctuary was easy to find. I'd stopped once or twice to ask directions. Usually when I ask someone the way, I inevitably pick a stranger to the area or a foreigner who doesn't speak English, or someone who is speech disadvantaged, but this time it was different. Not only did each person I spoke to know about the sanctuary but they all wanted to tell me about the dog they'd re-homed last week or the starving cat they'd rescued or the pony they'd adopted. I felt comforted to know that it is enduringly true that the majority of British people do love animals.

I parked and walked up the drive. There was no doubting that I'd arrived at the right place. There were ponies and donkeys in the fields, goats bleating, chickens clucking about the yard, dogs barking and everywhere I looked there seemed to be a different-coloured moggie.

Jenny Mark runs the sanctuary and she listened carefully while I told my tale. She is a tall, pretty girl in her early twenties with a mass of striking, long blonde and very curly hair.

'Oh yes, we have a lot of Rotties brought here. Big dogs, people get fed up with them. Or they can't afford to feed them.' I bent to fuss over a miniature Shetland pony; he was smaller than a dog.

Jenny told me that Rottweilers were her favourite breed. 'I remember the two you are talking about, Connie and King. Yeah. Lovely guys. Would you like to come into the office. I'll look them up.'

I followed her into a Portakabin where every spare inch of space was cluttered with dog baskets, leads, toys, pet info and adoption leaflets. There was a tiny chihuahua in a cage. It looked very thin. 'Just come in,' Jenny told me. 'She's in a bit of a state. I'm keeping her in here to keep my eye on her.' I put my hand out to stroke the little dog. It snapped and growled, baring sharp yellow teeth. 'She's going to bite the hand that feeds.' I snatched my fingers back just in time.

'She's been ill-treated,' Jenny explained. 'The dog wardens found her in a cellar.'

'Do you get many dogs brought in here?' I asked.

Jenny pushed her hair over her shoulders and smiled ruefully. 'We take all the stray dogs from the dog wardens. And those that have been thrown out, or knocked down, or injured.'

'By their owners?' I was shocked.

'Oh yes,' she told me. 'There are real horror stories. We get dogs in that have been hung from trees, or they've been used as footballs – they come in with smashed-up ribs and broken legs. If they get knocked down, people bring them here and we take them to the vet and get them patched up if we can.' Jenny was looking through a thick folder of doggy records. 'Sometimes they're just bags of bones when they come in. It's not unusual to get dogs that are too weak to stand because they've been starved.'

I shivered. 'It must be awful, having to deal with this.'

Jenny nodded. 'It is sometimes. Too sad.'

She told me about the puppy that had died in her arms only that week. The pony that came in because it had been blinded. The much loved elderly dog and cat whose 86-year-old owner had passed away.

'We do what we can,' she said. 'And there are a lot of happy endings as well.'

'Do you ever ...?' I didn't know how to phrase the question.

'Put dogs to sleep?' Jenny was shocked. 'Never,' she told me emphatically, 'although it's a terrible struggle financially.' She looked at me expectantly and I began fishing for my cheque book right away. 'We always manage to keep them somehow, even the elderly dogs, they like it here,' she said simply.

It was a real relief to know Connie and King hadn't been sent on their final journey to the canine Valhalla. But where were they? Surely Jenny would know if they were still at the sanctuary.

'Here they are.' She'd found their entry in the record book. 'Yes, I remember now. I saw the lady when we took them in.'

'Ah. Dorothy Tyler?'

'Yes, that's right. A Southerner. A bit of an accent. A very pretty lady. Loved her dogs. She was heartbroken when she went.'

'So, why did she leave them?' I couldn't understand it.

Jenny tried to remember. 'We see so many people, but I think she'd come to work up here and she thought she could have the dogs. That's it, she was managing a tourist centre, log cabins for holidays, that sort of thing. And she said it was in a wood and she thought she could keep the dogs.'

'But she couldn't?'

'No. She said they didn't behave themselves. King kept chasing sheep and I don't think the job worked out anyway. She told me that she couldn't settle.'

'What happened to the dogs ... do you still have them?'

Jenny shook her head. 'Connie was a lovely puppy. A skin complaint but we got her right and ...' She turned over to another page. 'We re-homed her to a lovely couple in Hathersage. A country home and we've heard from them, she's doing well.' Jenny smiled.

'And King?' What had happened to him?

'The lady came back to fetch him. She said she'd missed him too much. She found out that she couldn't bear to be parted from him. She said she was going back down south to try to make a new life for herself.'

I was pleased about that but I knew that the first thing Roy would want to know would be whether his sweetheart was married or with someone. I asked Jenny.

'I don't think so. She was on her own every time she came here. I didn't see a fella with her.'

There was a commotion outside ... a car had pulled up in the drive and we could hear a girl shouting.

Jenny rushed to the door. 'Oh, oh. The vet's here. We're castrating a colt this morning.'

I gulped. That was something I didn't want to stay around to see. The girl's cries suddenly turned to blood-curdling yells. 'Looks like someone's having problems.' Jenny muttered. She pulled on a padded jacket. 'We've had a Japanese Akita come in and he's a bit bolshie. He thinks the cats are lunch. I'd better go.'

'Just a minute.' I hadn't found out the most important thing yet. 'You couldn't give me Dorothy's address, could you?'

But it was mayhem outside. The Akita had chased after a cat, dragging his young handler into a rose bush in the process. A lorry had pulled up into the yard to deliver horse feed. The dog warden was unloading an emaciated-looking spaniel from the back of his van and there was a frazzled lady with a pushchair, three very young, tearful-looking children and a rabbit in a basket.

'Could you leave your number on the desk,' Jenny called out. 'I'll look it up and I'll give you a ring. Is that OK?'

I left her a donation, my mobile number and my land line and left the chaos behind. Jenny was obviously a capable and resilient girl and I had no doubt that she would cope brilliantly. And I felt elated. I set off for home. Wait 'til I told Roy.

The trail for Dorothy had been full of twists and turns and dead ends, but we were back on the case. She was in the south of England, she was unmarried, she still had her dog and I hoped to have some good news for him very soon.

CHAPTER 20

SHOTGUN WEDDING

EVERYBODY LOVES A WEDDING, BUT WHEN JOEY
PYLE TIED THE KNOT IT WAS A LITTLE BIT MORE
EXCITING THAN NORMAL. The ceremony itself was
held in Las Vegas and, as a lifelong friend, Roy was invited.
That led to trouble straight away.

Sheriff's Department, Las Vegas
Clark County, Nevada

10 April 2002

It is hereby noted that Mr Royston Shaw caused an
affray at Caesar's Palace on 19 March 2002. A claim
has been submitted by Mrs Edith Long of Fairfield
Road, Bow, London, England, for loss of amenity

and enjoyment of her holiday caused by the aforesaid Mr Shaw. The claim has been submitted by Mrs Long against Caesar's Palace in the sum of £50,000 and this, in turn, has been subrogated against the defendant Mr Shaw. Mr Shaw will be required to attend the Nevada County Court on 14 June 2002 at 2.30pm. It is strongly recommended that he obtains a lawyer to defend himself (we can provide details of suitably qualified lawyers should it be required). It is further pointed out that failure to attend the Court on that day or settle the claim prior to that date will result in a federal arrest on re-entry to the United States of America and the appropriate custodial sentence applied. Acknowledgement of this service is required in writing by return.

Sherrif's Department

Roy was back in this country, but had he left America of his own free will or had he been chucked out?

The wedding celebrations were still going on and I was on my way to meet him at Chelsea Football Ground where Joey and his blushing bride were having a 'bit of a do'.

It promised to be the gangster wedding party of the year, with gangsters flying over from America to have a knees-up with Joey and his lovely lady and their counterparts in this country – the cream of the London underworld. It was certainly going to be a wedding reception with a difference.

For this sort of a top-notch do, only the best is good enough. The cabaret had been flown in from Vegas and everyone would be out to make a good impression. I knew that I would have to put on a bit of style; if there was ever a time for the Versace dress, this was it. Leo was suited and booted, double-cuff shirt, gold cufflinks, silk tie and crocodile shoes.

I'd had my nails painted and my hair was sleek and shiny and straight from the salon – we were on our way. I wore my sheepskin slippers in the car; I was going to slip into my black suede stilettos at the last minute. Leo had his jacket on a coat hanger in the back of the motor. We were going to meet the 'Who's Who' of gangsterland; these are straight-up guys and the creased and crumpled look is a definite no-no. It wouldn't do to be anything less than immaculate.

Everybody makes a tremendous effort to look their best; the girls had been on the sunbed and at the hairdresser's with their rollers in and getting their roots done. They wouldn't set a foot out without the full works – high heels, dangly gold jewellery and lipstick, powder and paint.

As we pulled in the car park, I'd never seen so many flashy cars – Rollers, Mercedes, Bentleys, one or two Ferraris. The gangsters were stepping out of their status-symbol motors, and you could tell them straight away – it's the way they shrug their shoulders and pull their necks to get all that high-living fat out of their collars.

The dress code is as rigid here as at any society bash, all the men were dressed the same – crisp white shirts, top-pocket hankies, chunky 22ct rings on their pinkies. This was the 'do' to be seen at. They had all turned out for the man himself – Mr Joey Pyle – and they were ready to rock 'n' roll.

I pulled the sun visor down in my car, touched up my lipstick and fluffed up my hair. I turned to Leo. 'Do I look all right?' I asked him. 'No panty lines showing?' He gave me a push, told me I looked smashing and we went in. I have to say that gangster weddings, and gangster funerals, come to that, are not really my scene. I try to avoid them if it's at all possible, but the reason I was here was because it was Joey who'd asked me and it would have been a liberty to turn him down and also because everybody there would know Roy Shaw. These people have known him for years and seen him in action. It was an opportunity to talk to some of the top gangsters in the country. They'd normally clam up at interviews but here I wouldn't have to worry about them not wanting to talk to me; they were amongst their own, relaxing and having a jolly-up.

I took a deep breath and went in. The room was packed, there was lots of hugging, shaking hands and a buzz of conversation.

I saw a sprinkling of famous faces from the telly; it had to be *EastEnders* – they were well represented – Billy Murray, Steve Gafney and Pepe had turned up to see Joey and enjoy themselves. Everybody seemed to be looking towards the door to see if anyone more important was coming in.

It was a lovely spread, the caterers had done him well, salmon and cucumber, vol-au-vents, lobsters – all on huge platters. Waiters and waitresses wearing special outfits were hovering round, handing out food and drinks. The band played and the bar was bustling. 'Vodka and tonic, a large one, that'll do me ...' – everybody had a drink in their hand.

Geezers stood to one side of the room, dolly birds with next-to-nothing on sitting down at the other. I wanted to sit down as well, my feet were killing me.

Roy was on good form, catching up with old friends. The girls were all chatting about their man – ' 'Ere, 'ave you seen who he's with lately? What do you think about so and so, I reckon he's knocking her off ... Ooh, don't let his wife hear, oh quick, she's coming, look, hang on ... Hello, darling, how are you? How are you getting on with him now? He's better, is he?' As the woman looks away, they turn their heads and whisper, 'Oh, bless her heart, she waited 12 years for him. Do you know that? On his last long sentence.'

On the table in front of them were half-drunk gin and tonics and key fobs all jostling for position. Mercedes Benz, BMW, Lexus. Gone are the days of fur coats and no knickers – now their status depends on the car – whether it's a Toyota Land Cruiser or a 500SL. You hear more chit chat about cars from these gangster women than you do at the Motor Show. 'Do you have a convertible, darling? Ooh! He must be doing well. When's yours get out then?' Miaow, miaow. Scratch, scratch.

I glanced across at the bar at all these high-rolling blokes – there was no mistaking what they did for a living, with noses on one side of their faces and talking out of the corner of their mouths. Every now and then you'd see a little bob and a weave as they re-enacted a fight or a tear-up they'd had in one nick or another.

They were talking about their pals – 'Yeah, he's doing a ten ... Oh, he's doing life now, did you know that? ... Come round tomorrow, I've got a nice bit of work for ya.'

There was Joey, the king pin, in his best bib and tucker, holding court. He was the man in the chair tonight and he was loving it. Freddie Foreman was there and Charlie Richardson, all the famous names standing close by and hugging, tapping glasses, how are you doing, all the Don Corleone bit.

The next group of people were not quite in the top circle; they were good armed robbers, good blaggers, men that you could count on. 'Stand on him, he's a real good' un.' These were what they call 'staunch geezers'. Further out are the wannabees – they're bobbing in and out, trying to be useful. 'Can I get you a drink ... What's yours? ... What you having, Guv? ... Can I get you one, Fred?' These are the guys who hang around the top men and they've all come to pay their respects to Joe with presents under their arms. The bride still looked radiant as she sat at the head table with all her friends and family around her.

If only she knew what she'd taken on, what a life she has to come now. All the staying indoors, looking at the clock, waiting for him to come in, hoping he hasn't been nicked. She'll always need to keep the numbers of the barristers and solicitors at hand, ready for the tap at the door, just in case. I know ... I was that soldier.

I found myself standing next to Freddie Foreman at the bar; he was drinking a bloody Mary. He ordered me a lime and lemon and we pushed through the crowd to find a quiet space to have a chat. Freddie resembles a sinister character from a gangster film. He is softly spoken, his eyes stare unblinkingly. He's a man who has done what he's done and doesn't give a fuck who knows it. Freddie had a friendship with the Kray twins that stretched back over 40 years. He's known Roy nearly as long. He would be the first to admit that he'd lived by his wits for most of his life, thieving off the pavement as a young kid, progressing to full-time thieving and killing. Freddie was sentenced to 20 years in prison for murder and for disposing of Jack 'The Hat' McVitie's body after Jack had been murdered by the twins.

Freddie is an intelligent, articulate man who had told me previously that it would have been far easier to earn his money legitimately. There's nothing like a straight pound note. So what did he think about Roy?

'Roy is a tough guy – this is a rare breed. But when you meet Roy, you are in no doubt. He is courteous and polite. Roy has no need to be loud or threaten anyone.'

'Because he does the business?'

Freddie nodded. 'I've never known him target the ordinary man in the street. He'd go for anyone who crossed him, though.'

I knew that Freddie was a well-known boxer.

'I had over 40 professional fights,' he told me.

'Did you see any of Roy's matches?'

'Sure,' he nodded. 'I didn't miss them.'

'What was he like?'

Freddie thought about this for a moment. 'Awesome,' he told me simply.

'In what way?'

'He was pumped up, like a dynamo. He'd got a punch like a sledgehammer and he could box with both hands. That's what made him the most dangerous. His reputation went before him. Once he'd got going, there was no stopping him. It wasn't just the money, it was personal. He had to win.'

'Which boxer do you think he's most like?'

Freddie didn't hesitate. 'Tyson. They don't fight the same, but they both have the killer instinct. That's what you need to make it to the top.' Freddie finished his drink and nodded to a pal across the room.

'Just one more thing. Would you tell me a secret about Roy?'

He looked at me as though he thought I was mad.

'Not about jobs or anything. A little secret.'

Freddie smiled. 'I know they're making a film about Roy's life but, believe me, I've seen him do stuff you couldn't put on the screen. I couldn't tell you any of that ... he's one of the most ruthless men I've ever known. But at the same time, I've seen him with a tear in his eye. I don't know whether he'd mind me telling you – when one of his dogs died ... when he talks about his old mum ... and that girl he lost ...'

'Dorothy?'

'Yeah. I don't know why they ever split up.' A big man in a hand-made suit was tugging at his sleeve and he edged away. 'See you later, Katie,' he told me.

So Roy has a soft centre. Hmm. Who says tough guys don't cry?

I saw another tough guy, the host, Joey Pyle, standing on his own for a second by the buffet and I managed to corner him as he headed for the lobster. Joey has ruled the roost in the underworld for more than four decades, he is the original 'Teflon Don' – nothing sticks.

Everyone has heard of him, he is the most respected of them all but whether that's through fear or admiration, I can't be sure. Joey can move in any circle, whether it's royalty, celebs, MPs or murderers. And he knows more than a few of the latter. He's at ease with them all. Joey is, like Roy, a man of few words. There are similarities between them, both shrewd businessmen, both men you would be reluctant to approach without an introduction.

I asked Joey how long he'd known Roy.

'We go back a long way. I've seen Roy at his best and at his worst.'

'How do you mean?'

'There was no one to touch him when he was boxing. His fights were and still are legendary. He would have gone to the top if he'd boxed professionally.'

'And the worst?'

'I went to see him in Broadmoor. I'd heard that he was in a bad way. They had him on the punishment block.'

'Do you know why?'

Joey shrugged. 'It would be fighting. Prisons can't handle him.'

'I've heard, but Broadmoor?'

'I think that Roy found it harder than any prison. They kept him drugged, injecting him, he was barely conscious. They kept him so that he didn't know what he was doing. We had to do something.'

'Or he'd have ...'

'Yes, he was on a downhill slope. They were trying to turn him into a cabbage. They were killing him.'

'What did you do?'

Joey took a sip of his vodka. 'I had to do something that would bring him out of it – and also make them know he had friends. That we weren't going to sit back and let them destroy him.'

'You saved his life?'

Joey shook his head. 'No, he saved his own life. I might have helped a bit. I took a mate in to visit him. A high-profile boxer – Joe Louis.'

'Wow!'

'The Brown Bomber he was called. In those days, he was the equivalent of Mike Tyson. You can imagine if someone like Tyson was to come to this country and visit a bloke in prison, there'd be an almighty furore. And this is what happened. I took Terry Downs in as well.

'Broadmoor received a lot of publicity – and the Governor, he became a bit of a star. The main thing was it let everybody know that Roy Shaw was alive and kicking. I even took the Governor out for a night on the town.'

'Where'd you go?'

'The Astor Club in the West End.'

'Didn't he know about your reputation as a gangster?'

'He hadn't a clue who he was dealing with. I had to pick my moment. I asked him about Roy. He told me that, if Roy went on as he was doing, he'd be dead in a month.'

'Why were they doping him so much?'

'Because he was wild and uncontrollable. His own worst enemy at that stage. They were giving him the strongest injections every four hours that anyone could have and live. I knew I had to get him out of the punishment block and quickly.'

'How did you do that?'

'There was no chance that I could go to see him, but I got a mate of mine to visit. He was the owner of the Astor Club. He went and had a talk with him. I told him what to say, that he had to lay it on the line and spell it out for him. There were only two roads open to him at that time. He had to choose, to live or die.'

'He turned over a new leaf?'

Joey smiled. 'I wouldn't go so far as to say that, Kate. But he thought about it and saw that it made sense. Why throw your life away? He settled down. Decided to do his bird and get out. The rest is history.'

'How would you describe Roy?'

'He's one of the hardest men I've ever known, but he's fair. No one's going to take any liberties.'

'Do you know any secrets about him?'

'Secrets? You'd better ask him about them.' Joey waved to someone at the other side of the room. It was time for him to rejoin his party.

'He had a bit of a broken heart once, I don't know whether he's got over it,' Joey murmured, glancing across the room to where Roy was chatting up a glamorous young lady. She was leaning against the wall, smiling up at him and listening intently to whatever line he was throwing her.

Roy had his arms either side of her and was mesmerising her with those famous blue eyes. 'Maybe so.' Joey grinned as he excused himself and went back to mix and mingle with his guests.

Roy looked fantastic, 30 years younger than he should look. He was wearing a black-and-white silk dog-tooth shirt and a matching tie. His suit was Savile Row, wide-shouldered, navy-blue cashmere. Everybody wanted to know him, to buy him a drink and shake his hand.

Some of the old familiar faces were pale, grey-looking, as if they'd done a long stretch, a ten or a fifteen. They had lines on their faces, rugged and sad, faces that had been through the wars, they'd done a bit of acting, a bit of stabbing, a bit of shooting – and it showed. I could pick out the men who had just come out. Their suits were old-fashioned, they looked immaculate but as though they'd been hanging in a wardrobe waiting for their owner to come out from a lie down. These guys had eyes that had seen it all, they had looked at four grey walls, their faces were ashen, etched in pain and loneliness and paranoia. When they weren't looking around, they stared straight ahead and a little bit of 'if only'. Their age showed in their faces, they've lived every minute, every hour, every day of their sentence.

They seemed uncomfortable and awkward, as though the transition from prison to this was too hard to make, but this is the only world they know. I don't think any man in the room hadn't done time and most had done a long stretch. I have to say that crime doesn't pay, but it's ever so popular. The younger guys were trying to impress, making lots of noise, jumping around, doing a bit of gear, they were everyone's friend, but little dogs bark and big dogs bite. Sometimes these men are more dangerous because they have a reputation to make. These are circles that you cannot enter without an invite. This is a closed shop, they're very limited and rigid. The young upstarts would do anything to get in, they are constantly trying to prove themselves, to be accepted. The older gangsters all have books in their car, everybody has a story to tell and a bestseller to prove it.

As I stood there with Roy and all the top-notch gangsters, it seemed that everybody wanted to get into our circle. The band was playing '60s hits and the party was going with a swing. The Las Vegas cabaret was due to start, there was going to be a right old knees-up later on, but all I could think about was that the high heels had been a big mistake, my feet were killing me! Most of the chatting had been got out of the way and the gangsters were doing their duty, they were just about to cut the rug with their nearest and dearest. They left their key fobs on the table, so everyone could see what sort of car they had and who was doing well and who wasn't.

The underworld has changed. It's a different scene now, they seem to have a sense of openness. Perhaps it's the drug scene, but it seems easier for these people to get into this big-money, high-rolling world now. There were about 200 people at Joey's wedding bash, more than I expected. Most of them were millionaires but only a handful were in the same mould as Joe and Roy and Charlie and the rest. Perhaps the real gangsters are a dying breed.

I think that there will always be an underworld but that the younger blokes are plastic gangsters, and that there'll never be anyone like Joey Pyle, Freddie Foreman and Roy Shaw ever again.

CHAPTER 21

ONLY THE LONELY
PART TWO

WHEN ROY RANG ME UP AND INVITED ME OUT TO LUNCH, I DIDN'T KNOW WHAT TO EXPECT. It might be a table at The Ritz or the hamburger bar down the High Street. He'd sounded quiet on the phone. Had the wedding party made him realise what he was missing? Seeing other people's happiness might have brought his bachelor state home to him. I drove into London and rang him on his mobile phone.

'Where are we going then, Roy?' I asked.

'Nelson Street,' he replied. 'Meet me at Tubby Isaacs.'

Trust Roy always to do the unexpected. I'd not been to Tubby's for years. It's a favourite haunt of the real Eastenders and a bit of a tourist attraction these days, if you like jellied eels and pie and liquor, that is.

I parked the car and made my way to the café. It was

just the same as I remembered, red-and-white check plastic tablecloths, Eiffel Tower salt and pepper pots, lino on the floor and a chrome-and-formica counter top. Spotlessly clean and a mouthwatering smell of vinegar and freshly stewed eels. Roy came in, said 'Hello' and ordered for both of us. I wasn't sure about the eels but when they came they were delicious. I asked Roy if he'd enjoyed the wedding.

'Yes, it was all right,' he told me, dipping his bread in the gravy.

'Do you wish it was you?'

'Getting married?' He thought about it. 'There's not much chance of that, is there?'

'I don't know,' I told him. 'If you met up with Dorothy again ...?'

His eyes gleamed. 'Have you found her?'

I shook my head. 'Tell me a bit more about her. Where did you two first meet?'

'It was at a charity do. Eyes across the room, we looked at each other and just clicked. There was something about her.'

'Love at first sight.'

'That must have been it. I don't think I've ever felt the same about anyone else ever.'

'Did you two get together straight away?'

'No. I went to prison and we lost touch. I met up with her again when I came out.'

'Was she just the same?'

'She looked smashing, dark-brown hair, very pretty –

tall with lovely long legs. She's very clever, a bit posh but that didn't matter. Sometimes you're just on the same wavelength as someone; wherever we'd met, whatever our lives, it would have been the same. And that's how it was with her.'

'Soulmates?'

'Yes, we were.'

I wondered if Dorothy liked the same lifestyle as Roy. 'Did she enjoy pubbing and clubbing?

'That was part of the problem. Dorothy liked the simple things in life. She didn't need much to make her happy.'

'Did she like dogs?' This was a loaded question. I didn't want to raise Roy's hopes, but I had to know.

'Yes. Definitely. We had two Great Danes, an Alsatian and two Rottweilers. She loved the Rottweilers best. But she liked all dogs. We used to take them for a walk in the woods at the back of our house.'

'Did you live together?'

'She'd helped me with a bungalow I was renovating. I'd done all the hard graft, Dorothy had designed the interior. We lived there for some time.'

'Did she pick out the kitchen units?'

'Yes, and curtains and furniture. She did the decorating. It was fabulous when it was done.'

'Does she have good taste?'

'Excellent.' He nodded. 'She liked me, didn't she?' His face cracked into a grin but, at the same time, his eyes looked lonely. Bringing back memories isn't always such a good idea, even if they're happy ones. 'The place looked spectacular when it was finished. I had to give her credit for it.'

We'd finished our meal and I fetched two cups of tea from the counter.

'What went wrong, Roy?'

He looked down at his hands. 'It was my fault. I didn't know what I had. At that stage in my life, I was still wild. Dorothy was happy to go out for a meal and sit holding hands. But that wasn't my cup of tea. I'd been locked up for a long time and fighting was in my blood. My ideal night out was to go to a restaurant, then a show and on to a nightclub.'

'Did you get on all right apart from that?'

'Oh yeah. We used to go out driving, looking at country houses. I enjoyed it. We went to see Churchill's house, lots of mansions.'

'Didn't you like that sort of thing?'

'Yes, I did, actually. Things that she liked, I got to like. She was more mature. Ready to settle down. I wasn't. It was as simple as that.' Roy looked thoughtful. 'I had everything any man could want. At that time I was king of London, king of the Hill. I was a big man with all the respect and admiration anyone could want, the crowds all shouting my name. I had a pocket full of money and a lady who loved me.'

'Were you happy together?'

'I believed we were. She was my girl.'

'Were you ever jealous of her?'

Roy shook his head. 'She never gave me any reason to be. Dorothy is a lady. If you have her word, that's it.'

'So what went wrong?'

Roy frowned and took a deep breath. 'I don't really want to talk about it.'

'You have to now. If you want to find her. I must know what happened.'

Roy looked me straight in the eyes. 'OK. Looking back on it now, I was completely out of order. Dorothy helped me through all the hard times, when I was scraping for money, when I was building the house. She never complained. She worked alongside me, she stood by me through it all. I had it in the palm of my hand.'

'What?'

'Happiness,' Roy said simply. 'I threw it all away.' He held his hands up.

'What did you do?'

'I'd gone out on the razzle. And I met a young lady called Sharon. A pretty little thing. One thing led to another. I liked her.'

'Did you love her?'

'No, we've stayed friends. But there was nothing more to it than that.'

'Did Dorothy get to know you were cheating on her?'

Roy winced. 'Sharon had been going out with this other geezer and he knocked her about. So she asked me to do something about it.'

'And you did?'

'Of course. I finished up in court for it.'

'Did Dorothy know?'

'Not at that time. A mate of mine went to court with me and I had to have someone stand bail for me. He went and fetched Dorothy. That was the first she'd heard of it.'

'Poor girl. That must have been quite a shock.'

'When she found out what had been going on, it was all over between us.'

'You were working the doors at that time?'

'Yes, so I was out every night. Dorothy told me she was leaving but she couldn't move out straight away because she didn't have anywhere to go. So she stayed on, cleaning the house and doing the cooking for me.'

'That must have been hard for her.'

'Yeah, looking back on it, I was wicked to her, I tortured her. I was out every night messing about with the girls and she never said a word. We slept together but she asked me not to touch her and I didn't. She put her name down for a council house and in the end they gave her a one-bedroom flat.'

'She left then?'

Roy nodded. 'She cleaned the house from top to bottom before she went ... it was immaculate.'

'Was she upset when she left?'

'She cried. And I cried. I wanted her to stay.'

'Wouldn't she?'

'I'd hurt her too much. She'd made her mind up and that was it. I've never seen her to talk to her from that day to this.' Roy went very quiet, his face was pale and emotion was close to the surface. 'I must have broken her heart,' he said in a low voice.

We got up to leave. 'You both went your separate ways after that?' I said.

Roy held the door open for me. 'Yes, but I never stopped thinking about her. I've tried to find her. I once put an ad in the local paper – I took a full page, asking her to get in touch with me.'

'Nothing happened?'

'Maybe she didn't read it that week. She might have been living somewhere else.'

That fitted with what I knew.

Roy went on. 'Every other girl I've been with, I've always been straight with them. I've told them that the love of my life is Dorothy.'

I thought to myself, I bet that went down like a lead brick, but I didn't say it. 'Do you compare them to her?'

'Always. You see, Katie, I've settled down now. I've got money in the bank, everything anyone could want but I've no one to share it with. I only realised how much I loved her after I'd lost her.'

We stood on the pavement, it was grey and cold, the street was shiny, it had been raining and a few spots were still falling. I pulled my coat collar up, it was only a short walk to my car – Roy and I were parked in opposite directions but he didn't seem to want to go.

'And you've never seen her since?'

'I saw her that time at the petrol station. Then once when I was living at Epping. She was walking her dogs. She always loved dogs.'

That was something they had in common. 'Were they Rottweilers?' I asked.

'Yes.'

I started to walk away, but something about my voice must have made him pause. He caught hold of my sleeve.

'What would happen if you found her?' I asked him directly.

'Everything's different now. I'm looking for a partner and she would be the dream partner for me.'

It was raining harder now and I began to feel cold. Roy was like a dog on a scent, he wouldn't let me go.

'Say, you could find out where she is. You could talk to her again. If there was one thing you could say to her,' I asked him, 'what would it be?'

He didn't hesitate. 'I'd ask her to marry me. I'd say I was sorry for what had happened. I'd tell her that I wanted us to spend the rest of our lives together. We could go on holidays, all over the place, anywhere she wanted.'

I looked straight into Roy's blue eyes. I had no doubt that he was totally sincere. Had I found his secret at last? His Achilles heel. His one weak spot. No man is an island, there is something even he needs after all.

This is a man with a big heart – and he's learned from his mistakes. It's been a long, hard, rocky road to success for Roy Shaw but he did it, he achieved almost everything he set out to do. Almost. I felt a lump in my throat as we stood there on the street corner. There was just one more thing he needed. Something money can't buy. If finding Dorothy would do it, I couldn't stand in his way. I fished in my coat pocket and pulled out a crumpled piece of paper. It had a few words scribbled on it in biro.

'A present for you, Roy,' I told him softly as I pushed it into his hand.

I walked off quickly, only turning to look back as I reached the corner. The rain had disappeared and the sun was peeping out from behind the clouds. A good omen. I watched Roy's face break into a huge smile, the years seeming to fall away as he read the paper.

'YE-E-ES!' he yelled, clenching his fist into a salute. I felt like yelling myself, I felt that good.

It was Dorothy's telephone number.

Roy Shaw's Career at Her Majesty's Pleasure

Wormwood Scrubs
Husk Borstal
Bristol
Lewes YP
Maidstone
Canterbury
Pentonville
Brixton
Wandsworth
Parkhurst
Grendon Underwood
Broadmoor
Gartree
Leicester
Hull
Durham
Birmingham
Oxford
Long Lartin
Colchester Army Prison
The Nut House in Germany
The Nut House in England